NUGAMENTA;

A BOOK OF VERSES

BY

GEORGE EDWARD RICE.

> " Nos triftia vitæ
> Solamur cantu." STATIUS.
>
> " I left no calling for this idle trade,
> No duty broke." POPE.

BOSTON:
J. E. TILTON AND COMPANY.
1860.

Riverſide, Cambridge:

Printed by H. O. Houghton & Co.

TO THE MEMORY OF ONE WHOSE GENTLE EYES WILL NEVER REST UPON THESE PRINTED PAGES, THEY ARE INSCRIBED, THOUGH ALL UNWORTHY OF THE HONOR, WITH SENTIMENTS OF AFFECTION AND REGRET THAT LANGUAGE CANNOT INDICATE NOR TIME DESTROY.

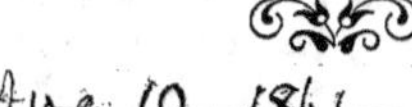

Aug. 10 – 1861 –

SUICIDE. We regret to learn that Mr. George Edward Rice shot himself yesterday in the boarding house of Mr. David Reed, Roxbury. Mr. Rice was well known in the community as a graceful poet, and both his serious and humorous productions have elicited much praise from competent judges. We have not learned the cause of the act, but suppose it must have been depression of spirits amounting to aberration of mind.

NUGAMENTA. A BOOK OF VERSES. By GEO. EDWARD RICE. Boston: TILTON & Co.

Between the highland of poetry and the prairies of prose lies a middle ground of verse, fit to be the chosen home of refined thought and graceful feeling, but not often very successfully occupied. There HORACE built his villa; and there the most charming of the writers to whom France concedes the honors of the muse abide. Our own English literature is less rich in such men, partly, perhaps, because the genius of the language lends itself less easily to their fine evanescent fancies, partly because the ways and passions of the race are too positive to give them much chance for existence. Yet WALLER belongs to their order, and no *salon* of Paris ever listened to a lighter thrumming of the spiritual guitar than passed from the facile fingers of PRAED.

In America few have essayed this mid-region of music and feeling with so much success as Dr. HOLMES; and now Boston sends us, in the person of Mr. GEORGE E. RICE, another New-England candidate for honors which the heirs of the cavaliers might have been supposed more likely to grasp than the sons of the Puritans. Mr. RICE'S *Nugamenta* is a book which none but a gentleman could have written, full of delicate perceptions, fleeting gleams, and glooms as fleeting, quaint conceits and honorable sentiments. They have been clothed in metre with no unskillful hand, and the writer is over-modest when he offers them to the *uncritical* reader alone as the possible solace of worn or weary hours.

PREFACE.

This Book contains a few pieces of occaſional Verſe, which, without pretenſion to Poetry, the writer truſts may beguile ſome weary moments for the uncritical reader.

April, 1860.
16 Court Street, Boston.

CONTENTS.

SONNETS.

L'ENVOI.

VERSES.

THE PROPHECY.

PART I.

If you would hear me ſpeak of one who dwelt
In that fair land of Poland, years agone,
And of his fate, ſo mournful, — and would hear
Alſo of one whoſe love and grief for him
Raiſed her from Earth to Heaven — Liſten!

There are ſuch things, however worldlings ſneer,
As love for all mankind, and ſympathy
With every ſuffering of humanity, —
As loftineſs of purpoſe in a life, —
As moral grandeur in a death, that crowns
A peerleſs life with an immortal fame, —
As Woman's love, through ſorrow and diſtreſs, —
As truſt unfaltering, and as broken hearts.

The moon was flooding with her gentle light
The green and dewy meadow, and ſhe made

The night ſo calm and lovely, lovelier ſtill;
The ſtars, o'erpowered by her brighter beams,
Scarce ventured forth, ſave here and there a few
That faintly glimmered in the Orient.
Nature ſeemed tranquil, — not a breeze ſwept by
To bid the lily rear its coronal,
Or waft its perfume from the violet;
And ſave the murmuring of the rivulet,
That, creeping ſluggiſhly along, illumed
By calm Diana's rays, ſeemed molten ſilver,
The ſilence was unbroken; till a ſound,
That ſeemed the meaſured tread of warlike men,
Came from a wooded and far-diſtant hill;
Nearer it came, and nearer; now the moon
Gleamed on the bayonets, and touched their points
With her pure argent light, and now they came
With ſlow and ſteady ſtep acroſs the plain
Straight to the river's margin. All were armed
Save one, who trod the proudeſt and moſt firm,
Though he alone of all had nothing more
To hope on earth, — for he had come to die.
His crime was this: He dared to ſtand alone
The champion of the Suffering and the Poor;
He thought that human laws might yet be framed
More equal for the Lowly and the Great;
And that God made this fair and beauteous Earth
So beautiful, for all men to enjoy
And walk erect thereon in majeſty.

They called it Treafon, when he fpake thefe thoughts,
And led him forth upon the plain to die, —
To die at night, — this calm and lovely night, —
Becaufe beneath God's glorious eye, — the Sun, —
They dared not kill the man the people loved.

Erect and unappalled he ftood ; his eye,
Bright with the light of genius and of truth,
Undimmed, could face Death's cruel meffengers.
Godlike he feemed in beauty and in mien ;
Young, valiant, noble, and yet doomed to die, —
His purpofe unaccomplifhed, and his great
And lofty deftiny yet unfulfilled.
He looked upon the fky, the moon, the ftars,
The river and the meadow he muft leave
In one brief moment ; and he thought of Him
Who made them all fo grand and beautiful,
And breathed a prayer that he might find at laft
Reft in His kingdom ; then he thought of her —
The flower he had worn upon his heart
In all its bloom, its fragrance, and its beauty —
Whofe calm fweet fmile was ever at his hearth,
Whofe life was love and gentlenefs and peace,
And with her name upon his lips he gave
The fatal fignal. Oh, moft worthy he,
Living, to live in fome true woman's eyes,
And, dying, to be buried in her heart !

A quick, ſharp volley, then a heavy fall,
And all was over.
Oh, 'twas bravely done!
Io Triumphe! 'twas a worthy deed!
Now ſound the bugle, beat the rattling drum,
And back to whence ye came. Go! leave the corſe,
That held the ſoul that God is keeping now,
A prey to wolves leſs mercileſs than ye.

PART II.

Alas, how ill news ſpeeds! And yet ſhe knew,
Ere they had told her, that her Love lay dead!
Between two great and loving hearts the bond
Of ſympathy is ſuch, though ſeas divide,
One cannot bleed alone. She ſhed no tear
And made no moan, but ſhe aroſe and wrapped
Her mantle 'round her ſlender form and fled
Straight to the bloodſtained ſod, — for Love inſpired,
And they whom Love inſpires can ne'er be wrong.
The moon, that hid her face behind a cloud
And would not ſee him die, ſhone forth to light her.
Onward ſhe came with ſwift unſteady gait,
Springing, then faltering, like a wounded deer; —
Right on ſhe ſped to his pale corſe, direct
As ſteel flies to the magnet. When ſhe ſaw
The outline of his figure, where he lay

As graceful and as beautiful in death
As e'er in life, there rofe one piercing fhriek,
Wild and unearthly, that might rend the fky;
Yet on fhe came. O God! what human power
Could keep thefe hearts apart! Ah! never yet
Had Love a truer votary than fhe.
She reached the fpot and knelt, — fhe could not weep, —
Her eyes feemed balls of fire, and her heart,
Throbbing convulfively with painful fobs
All unrelieved by tears, was breaking now.
She wound her arms around his form, and fpake
To him who ne'er before refufed to liften: —
"Kind friend, fond lover, gentle hufband, fpeak!
It is your Wenda calls. How oft you've faid,
When fitting fide by fide fome fummer's eve,
Your arm around me, that if you were dead
My kifs would roufe you. There, my fweet Love, there!
I prefs my lips fo cold to yours ftill colder;
My arms are 'round you; are you dead, quite dead?
Is the heart ftilled whereon my head hath lain
So calm and fweetly tranquil, all unmoved
Save by its throbs that fyllabled my name?
My Love, my Life, my Lord, will you not fpeak?
My bofom ever thrilled at your dear voice
Like harpftring to the minftrel's touch. Oh, speak!
My inmoft thoughts were yours, and every wifh

Of my fond heart, and all my Fancy's dreams ;
You were my firſt, my laſt, and only Love,
And all my ſpirit was by yours controlled.
And are you dead, my own ſweet Love, quite dead ?
So good, ſo noble, generous, and brave !
You will not ſpeak. I ſeem of ſenſe bereft —
My brain is reeling. Hark ! I hear a voice
Not yours, my Love. It is the cry of Blood !
For blood unjuſtly ſhed, blood ſtill muſt anſwer."

Then roſe ſhe from his ſide, and ſtanding forth
Towered a Pythoneſs in majeſty.
She turned her face towards Warſaw, and ſhe raiſed
Trembling aloft one ſmall and ſculptured hand
As white as alabaſter, ſave a ſpot
Made crimſon by a gallant heart's beſt blood,
And thus ſhe ſpake : —
"Woe to the Capital !
To the Kingdom, woe ! I feel the ſpirit
Of prophecy is on me. Woe to Poland !
A century ſhall paſs, then there ſhall be
The Ruſſian in your homes. I hear the ſhriek
Of dying victims, and I ſee the light
Of blazing roofs. Woe to fair Poland, woe !
This noble blood ſhall be avenged in time."
Then fell ſhe on the corſe, and there ſhe lay,
Her breaking heart againſt his broken one,
Murmuring ſo gently, — "Let me die with him

I loved ſo much ! O Father, let me die !"
And God was merciful and heard her prayer.

A century has paſſed, and that fair land
Is known no more 'mid nations of the world.
The Ruſſian at their hearths and in their halls
Now reigns ſupreme, yet Nature is the ſame ;
The meadow ſtill is fair, the moon beams bright,
The rivulet creeps by, and nought ſeems changed,
Unleſs, perchance, one bank of violets
Is of a brighter and a lovelier hue
And yields a ſweeter perfume, for it grows
Above two noble hearts, and there for aye
The moon ſhall beam, the rivulet creep by.

FANTASIA.

When I, in melancholy mood,
By real or by fancied griefs oppreſt,
Sigh but for peace and long to be at reſt,
I find it good
Alone to wander
Far from the crowded mart and walks of trade,
Where foot of man hath ſeldom trod,
And there in ſolitude and ſilence ponder
On all the works of a moſt bounteous God.
I ſeek ſometimes the Foreſt ſhade ;
To the ſad muſic of the Pines I liſten,
And watch the wild wood flowers,
With hues made brighter by the grateful ſhowers,
Wave in the wind and in the ſunlight gliſten ;
Or by the margin of the boundleſs ſea,
The ſhore my couch, the Heaven my canopy,
Reclining on the ſand I lie
To hearken to the ripple's mournful tune,
Or by the ſilvery radiance of the moon
To mark the gorgeous pomp and splendors of the
ſky.

While ſtraying thus one day
From all the haunts of men
Far, very far away,
To greet the breezes from acroſs the ſea,
I came upon a ſmall and lovely glen
Where grew the Jaſmine and the Violet,
The ſpicy Pink, the fragrant Mignonette,
And ſweet Anemone ;
And in that lonely ſpot,
With Woodbine covered o'er,
Stood a ſequeſtered cot.

Wearied and faint, and tired of meditation,
I hailed with joy this human habitation,
And at the cottage door
I ſaw a man with flowing ſilvery hair
Who beckoned me to come, and placed a chair
And aſked me to partake his ſimple fare.

Refreſhed with food and wine,
I thanked this hoſt of mine ;
And when I roſe, my footſteps to retrace,
Sadly the old man ſighed,
And the big tears came ſtreaming down his face.
"You've been by ſorrow tried, —
Tell me your tale," I cried,
"Why by this deſolate ſhore,
Hearing the wind's ſad moan

And the deep ocean's roar,
You dwell remote, untended, and alone."

Sadly he gazed on the glorious ſea,
And this was the tale as he told it to me : —

"Long, long ago in years gone by,
Ere ſorrow ſtruck me with a fatal dart,
And Life was bright and hopes were high,
I wooed and won the Idol of my heart.

"In this little cot lived we,
That gentle girl and I,
As happy as we could be.
Week after week flew by,
Flew by my Love and me,
And month came in and month paſſed out,
But we heeded not what the months were about
So pleaſantly lived we
By the ſide of the ſounding ſea.

"Happy beyond humanity's lot
Were we in this deſolate ſpot,
For ſwiftly and joyouſly paſſed the time
While we read volumes of quaint old rhyme
Sung by the Poets whoſe wonderful art
Quickens the throbs of a Nation's heart,
And thoſe enchanting tales of Fairy land

That erſt had charmed us in our childhood's hours;
And then, with hand in hand,
Or with my arm around her ſlender waiſt,
Happy to be thus placed,
We wandered o'er the fields and plucked the flowers.

"Thoſe days have flown, — I can but ſay 'Woe's
me!'
And think how blithe were we;
Unmindful that calamity might come;
That we might live and love no more
In our ſmall cot, beſide this rocky ſhore,
That made ſo dear a home.
We could not fancy as the years flew by, —
Flew by on angel's pinions, —
That any clouds could darken our bright ſky;
That aught could dim the luſtre of an eye
Or cauſe one tearful ſigh
In Love's dominions.

"How oft at eve, along the rocks, we ſtrolled
To hear the ocean's roar
And watch the waves, as one by one they rolled
Up the reſounding ſhore!
And as we recognized the mighty hand
Of Him who made the ſea, the ſky, the land,
We felt our ſouls expand,
And loved each other more
Than e'er we loved before.

" So love went on increafing day by day,
And three years paffed away ;
No happier hours were ever known than we
Enjoyed in this fmall cot befide the deep blue fea.

" One fearful night,
When the ftorm was abroad in all its might,
Reading I fat alone
Hearing the moan
Of the fierce tempeft, and the ocean's roar,
And by our cottage door
Swept the great angry waves with many a groan
And many a difmal wail ;
Frequent the lightning's flafh,
Frequent the fudden crafh,
That told of fome great tree laid proftrate by the gale.

" She in the funfhine of whofe fmile I lived,
In winning whom Life's purpofe feemed to end ;
Who never, while I loved her, could have grieved, —
My better angel and unchanging friend, —
Had feen the heavy clouds around us lower
And fought her chamber at the twilight hour ;
But when the ftorm rofe high
And raged with violence fo fuperhuman
I wifhed to join her, — for, when danger's nigh,
'Tis thought a gentle woman
Feels lefs inquietude and fear,
If by her fide is one to whom fhe's dear, —

So I the half-read book
Returned to its accuſtomed nook
And ſought the chamber where I thought there lay
All that my God had given, — all he could take away.

"Softly I opened the unfaſtened door;
She who remembered every ſacred duty,
In all her innocence and beauty,
Was kneeling on the floor.
I knew her prayer aſcended,
Meekly, ſincerely,
For him ſhe loved ſo dearly,
And, ere that prayer was ended,
For me to enter there
Would have profaned the air
Made holy by her prayer.
I could but worſhip her, —
A ſaintlike woman who could never err, —
So ſtainleſs and ſo fair.

"When her fond prayer was ſaid
She raiſed her queenlike head
And turned on me her gentle eyes
With a faint ſmile of ſweet ſurpriſe.
Forth from the threſhold of the door
I sprang to raiſe her from the floor,
But ere my extended arms
Could claſp her graceful charms

A ſudden, dazzling glare
Lightened the murky air,
And on the floor ſhe lay ;
Without a ſigh or groan
Her ſoul had paſſed away
And I was left — alone !

"Stilled is the heart that ſolely beat for me
Three happy years beſide the deep blue ſea ;
The gentle eyes are cloſed
That ſhone ſo brightly when I ſang their praiſes,
And o'er the boſom where my head repoſed
Grow now the violets and daiſies.
There, in her favorite dell,
Where ſhe oft wandered when the Morn was break-
ing,
She ſleeps the ſleep that knows no waking,
Surrounded by the flowers ſhe loved in life ſo well.

"Long years have fled ſince then,
And Time has bowed my head and blanched my hair,
While I, remote from men,
Have paſſed my days in ſtudy and in prayer.
Here in this ſpot made holy by her death
Will I yield up my breath,
And while I live my life ſhall be
Kept ſacred to her memory.

'Tis good to bear the Crofs,
And if my grievous lofs
To me is fanctified,
And I, by fore affliction tried,
From all my earthly taints
And fins am purified,
In manfions of the Juft,
Beyond the fky, I truft
To meet her with the Saints."

The fun had tinged the weftern wave with glory,
The twilight had crept on me, and the pall
Of Night had flowly fettled over all,
The while I liftened to this tearful ftory;
Then through the air I heard a diftant bell
That pierced my foul like a funereal knell,
And I aroufed me and my footfteps bent
Homeward in ferious and thoughtful mood,
With all my feelings chaftened and fubdued,
On the philofophy of dreams intent.

WHAT MIGHT HAVE BEEN.

" For of all ſad words of tongue or pen,
The ſaddeſt are theſe, — 'It might have been.'"

WHITTIER.

I.

WHAT lies in the ſhadowy Future, alas !
Never falls within a blind Mortal's ken ;
We cannot foreſee what will come to paſs,
But we know too ſurely what might have been ;
Fulfilment of hopes that our ſanguine youth
Thought ſimply awaited that we ſhould be men
And could buckle our armor on for the Truth
Are among all the things that might have been.

II.

Like miſt in the morn fled the roſeate hue
Everything wore in that cloudleſs day
When hearts beat gayly, for Life was new
And flowers ſeemed ſcattered all over our way ;
We thought the time of our triumph ſo proud
Would come and denote us victorious men,
Now nameleſs we ſtruggle amid the crowd
And bitterly think of what might have been.

III.

Sorrow is fruitleſs, — Regret is vain, —
Experience teaches but little to man ;
We ſhould neglect our chances again,
Though we now know ſomething of Nature's plan ;
We talk of the blind undiſcerning Age
That hailed us not as the coming men, —
Hiſtory opened a virgin page
To receive our names, — did we ſeize the pen ?

IV.

Ah, no ! we baſked and dreamed in the ſun
While opportunities rare went by,
We awoke to find that nothing was done,
Then ſat us down in the duſt to ſigh ;
We grieve, when we are alone to blame,
We, the vainglorious, cowardly men, —
Not having conquered a wreath from Fame,
It is idle to prate of what might have been.

V.

But yet to us all 'tis the ſolace left,
When diſappointment has marked our way,
Being of hope for the Future bereft,
To ſpeak of the hope of a former day ;

Not having been to our Miſſion true,—
  And heaven ordains to the leaſt of men
Manifold duties that he ſhould do,—
  We love to talk of what might have been.

VI.

I might have roamed over this world ſo wide,
  In happineſs ſuch as ne'er mortal knew,
I as your guard, and you as my guide,
  In ſearch for the Beautiful, Pure, and True;
I might have won an undying fame,
  That would live in the hearts of my fellow-men,
And have made you proud that you bore my name:
  All theſe are things that might have been.

VII.

My youth was tinged with a golden hue,
  By the fond illuſion that you were mine,
That I ſhould prove my paſſion was true,
  By a life's devotion through ſtorm and ſhine.
We might have been happy — but let that paſs,
  For naught betides that we hoped for then,—
You are ſleeping under the waving graſs,
  And I live but to think of what might have been.

ATARAXIA.

WHEN I am all aweary of the ſtrife,
The turmoil and the reſtleſſneſs of life,
And can no longer bear my unquiet heart
By cares and fears diſtreſt,
But need the ſolace and the balm of reſt,
I leave the town with all its buſy hum
And ſeek the country and its ſolitude ;
Here to theſe fields I come,
And need no Teacher with his formal art
To prove that man is nought and God is good, —
No voice can ſpeak like Nature's to my heart ; —
In every leaf and bud and flower I ſee
How great His power, and feel how weak are we ;
And as beſide this violet bank I lie
Marking the ſtream glide by
With ſteady ceaſeleſs flow,
Myſelf I ſcarcely know ;
I am no longer he who came
In fierce deſpairing mood
With all his brain aflame,
But I am tranquil, quiet, and ſubdued ;

For as the ſtream flows onward to the ſea,
With gentle murmur ſoothing my ſad ſoul,
It bears my gloomy thoughts far, far from me,
And off my heart the heavy ſhadows roll.

And while beſide this river's brink
I lie ouſtretched, I think
How true it is we ſuffer not alone, —
Of griefs we know our own,
But be he friend or brother
We know not all the ſorrows of another;
And ſome who act a cheerful part
Have ſome great hidden grief
From which there's no eſcape — to which there's
no relief,
That like a vulture rends the bleeding heart,
Who yet will not complain,
And ne'er betray,
Coſt what the ſtruggle may,
By any outward ſign, the inward pain.

It is the inevitable law
That man is born to trouble and to ſorrow,
And uncomplaining he ſhould bear the croſs,
For if each to-morrow
Brings not the ſolace that we hope to-day,
Nor makes atonement for ſome bitter loſs,
It ſets us farther on our onward way,

And leaves us nearer to that pleaſant ſhore
Where care and grief can trouble us no more.

Then whatſoe'er the Fates decree,
It ſtill ſhall be
The conſtant burden of my prayer and ſong
That I may have the power
In ſtern Misfortune's hour,
To ſuffer and yet evermore be ſtrong.

TO GLYCERA.

I.

After ſo long a thraldom, to be free,
Is happineſs ſupreme. I once ſuppoſed,
My pulſe could never throb, except for thee;
Thou wert my heart's true Queen, but now, de-
poſed
By thy rebellious ſubject, who at laſt
Brooks not the Tyrant. Go, thy reign is paſt!

II.

Though all is over, and 'twere worſe than idle
The aſhes of this buried love to raiſe,—
Yet thoughts come thronging, and I cannot bridle
The tongue that ſang ſo often in thy praiſe;
The World was all forgotten for thy ſake;
And I muſt ſpeak, or my full heart will break.

III.

The recollection of the days now fled,
When all my thoughts were truſted to thy care,—

When I ſtill followed where thy footſteps led,
And deemed it happineſs thy griefs to ſhare,—
Shall, in the ſilent night, come back to thee,
And fill thy ſaddened heart with dreams of me.

IV.

And I, alas! muſt think and ſigh the while,
How, overcoming all my manhood's pride,
I hailed the ſunſhine of thy glorious ſmile,
And knew no pain, but abſence from thy ſide;
Apart from thee, this loving heart of mine
Throbbed the dull moments till my lips met thine,—

V.

And then my blood, with lava-flowing tide,
Courſing tumultuous through each ſwelling vein,
Swept like a torrent down the mountain ſide,
Straight to my burning ſoul and maddening brain;
And in thoſe hours of terrible unreſt,
I told the love that raged within my breaſt.

VI.

Thy lips reſponded, and my joyous heart
Leaped like a courſer, as he nears the goal;
My reaſon fled, o'ercome by Beauty's Art,
And I was thine at hazard of my ſoul.
Nay, ſpeak not! I have known by far too well,
Thy voice's muſic, and its magic ſpell.

VII.

But now, when Reaſon reaſſerts her ſway,
  I feel that Life hath nobler ends than Love,
The fond ambitious dreams of Boyhood's day
  Return, as to the Ark the wandering dove;
Hard is the ſtruggle, but I rend thy chain,
And ſtand erect. I am a man again!

VIII.

Enfranchiſed now, no more my ſteps ſhall ſtray
  To thine abode. We part at length forever!
I ne'er will let thy Siren voice eſſay
  To lure me back again. I ſwear, that never
Will I behold thee, leſt thy charms ſhould move
My lips to flatter, and my ſoul to love.

IX.

No more in trembling accents will I ſue,
  Or gather bloſſoms to bedeck thy head;
The Paſſion that I nurſed until it grew
  Stronger than Reaſon, now is cold and dead,
And cold and dead to thee ſhall be the heart
Once ſo controlled by thy tranſcendent Art.

X.

I grieve for mine own weakneſs; I rèpine
  At moments loſt in gazing on thy face;

I have regained my heart, that long was thine,
  By one ſtrong manly effort, and no trace
Of all my fond affection ſhall be ſeen ;
I will not be the ſlave that I have been.

XI.

We part ! Farewell ! I never can forget
  What it were better could Oblivion ſhroud ;
But will not pauſe to tell one ſad regret ;
  I'll breathe a ſigh, then onward with the crowd.
Is that a tear ? My ſtruggles are in vain ;
See, Love, I'm kneeling at thy feet again !

TWILIGHT AND MOONLIGHT.

TWILIGHT.

I.

THE twilight with its miſtineſs and gloom
  Over the peopled city ſlowly falls,
While I am ſitting in my lonely room
  Watching the ſhadows deepening on the walls.
Let me not think of viſions that have paſt, —
  Of hopes of Fame, — of ſtern demands of duty, —
Of Boyhood's dreams too ſanciful to laſt, —
  I'll take the hour to ſing of Love and Beauty.

II.

But ere the Lyre yields to my careſſing,
  Sweet ſtrains of muſic float upon the air,
A gentle hand is on my ſhoulder preſſing,
  I turn and ſee an angel by my chair.
"From yon blue Heaven," ſhe ſays, "I guard and cheriſh
  All thoſe who ſtrive to win the I oet's crown,
Be not enſlaved by Beauty or you periſh
  And fall from Godlike heights ignobly down."

III.

I dare to anſwer, and with accents trembling
Exclaim, "Let Fame depart, I'll not repine;
When Beauty ſmiles, my heart knows no diſſembling,
And what were Glory to a Love like mine!"
"Alas," ſhe ſays, "Has Reaſon then no chance?
Lift to her clarion voice for one brief minute;"
"Hold! hold!" I cry, "I'll break her ſhining lance,
For what is Love if there is Reaſon in it?"

IV.

Again ſhe ſpeaks, but now with exultation,
"Your heart, I find, is in the right condition;
'Tis Love that gives the Poet inspiration,
And power to fulfil his lofty miſſion;
Love on, — 'twill keep the heart forever young,
Hymn Beauty's praiſes whereſoe'er you're roving,
The nobleſt ſongs by Poet ever ſung
Were ſung by him who knew the pains of loving."

MOONLIGHT.

V.

And now Diana, from her throne on high, —
That virgin huntreſs with the ſilver bow, —

Becomes each moment brighter in the ſky,
 And ſheds her gentle light on all below ;
And through each pane within my caſement ſtream-
  ing,
 My room ſhe lightens with her beams divine,
It is the hour when a Poet's dreaming
 Is woven into verſe, and this is mine.

MYRRHA.

" She came in all her Beauty, like the moon from the cloud of the Eaſt. Lovelineſs was around her as light. Her ſteps were like the muſic of ſongs." OSSIAN.

I.

My Fancy now has taſked her utmoſt ſkill,
  And called before me an entrancing viſion
To ſoothe my heart, to charm away each ill,
  And lap me in a happineſs Elyſian;

II.

For I diſcern acroſs the moonbeams flitting
  A ſylphlike form of excellence moſt rare,
And now around the couch whereon I'm ſitting
  She floats in all her beauty through the air.

III.

I know within that form reigns Myrrha's heart,
  To none but her ſuch fabled charms are given;
Nature, for once, has far exceeded Art,
  And ſent her as a perfect work from Heaven.

IV.

I ſeize the Lyre, — in vain I ſtrive to ſing
The love my tongue to her would fain expreſs,
Her name alone breathes forth from every ſtring, —
My Art is conquered by her lovelineſs.

V.

The ſtrength, that I had vainly deemed my ſtay,
Melts like the ſnow before her Beauty's light, —
Her charms divine uſurp my mind by day,
And break repoſe with reſtleſs dreams by night.

VI.

In ſtore for me are many dreary hours,
But, Myrrha, there are none for one ſo fair;
Thy path ſhall be enamelled o'er with flowers, —
The Beautiful are God's eſpecial care.

AT THE FIRESIDE.

Come, deareſt, ere they light the evening lamps,
And ſit with me and gaze upon the fire.
I like to watch the dying embers fade;
Thus let my arm encircle thee; — now reſt
Againſt my ſhoulder thy dear queenlike head,
And I will tell thee how my wayward Life
Was unfulfill'd until I won thy love;
For my ſad ſoul was like the wandering dove
Sent from the Ark, that found no reſting place;
Or like ſome rudderleſs and ſhattered Bark
Forſaken on a wild tempeſtuous ſea,
Drifting its aimleſs courſe from point to point,
Fixed to no purpoſe. There were few to ſmile
And bid God ſpeed me on my onward courſe.
Life had for me nor object, end, nor aim;
All noble aſpirations, high reſolves
And fond ambitious dreams had fled. I ſeized
The flowery wreath that ſmiling Pleaſure held,
And liſtened to her Siren voice, nor ſtrove
To looſe the arms ſhe flung around my neck;
But all was Vanity, — and I grew weary

Of this ſad world of trouble, pain, and guilt.
Dark was my ſoul, but when the light of thine
Shone on me, I aroſe like ſome way-worn,
Benighted traveller, who perceives that Day
Is breaking in the Eaſt, and ſtruggles on
To greet the upriſing Sun. Before thy beams,
The clouds diſperſed, and life again ſeemed bright.
Taught by thy grand example then I learned
How dear and pleaſant are the ways of Truth.
I ſtrove to walk within her peaceful paths,
And Thou wert my exceeding great reward.

THE CROWNING MERCY.

I.

Fill up the cup, my Beauty, fill up,
We've a long way to travel before we can ſup ;
Your blue eyes are bright, and would they might light
The dangerous path we muſt travel to-night ;
Charlie has fled, there's a price on his head,
And many a gallant at Worceſter lies dead.

II.

If the cropheads advance, we ſhall forfeit the chance
To eſcape from theſe ſhores to luxurious France ;
Yet here we'll remain for a moment to drain
A flagon and ſing a wild cavalier ſtrain ;
Ere to ſaddle we ſpring theſe rafters ſhall ring
With death to Old Noll and long life to the King.

III.

Many times by the ſide of Rupert, our pride,
Have I had the honor in battle to ride ;
In Marſton Moor's fray, throughout all the day,
I ne'er from the ſound of his voice was away ;

At Nafeby's fight, I rode clofe to his right,
And helped him efcape by the fhade of the night.

IV.

But never, I ween, has fuch carnage been feen
In thefe wars as at Worcefter to-day there has been;
Through the gates, which they crafhed, the Puritans
    dafhed,
And bright in the funlight their morions flafhed;
Thus taken by ftorm, our troops couldn't form,
And the hand-to-hand conflict was bloody and warm.

V.

No mufic I hear is fo fweet to my ear
As the din of the conteft when weapons ring clear;
Our good fwords were tough, our greeting was rough,
And with crimfon we dyed many jerkins of buff;
Fierce battle we gave all the day, and the wave
Of Severn flowed red with the blood of the brave.

VI.

It was war to the knife, and through the hot ftrife
Each Cavalier knew that he fought for his life;
How fweet were the moans and the fhrieks and the
    groans
Of the knaves that our chargers' hoofs trod to the
    ftones;
By Jove! 'twas a fight, as to left and to right
We cut and we flafhed through that terrible fight.

VII.

By Charlie we ſtood while it did any good ;
But, when he had fled, we eſcaped as we could ;
The Country is loſt, — this we know to our coſt, —
And the boiſterous channel to-night muſt be croſt ;
For ſucceſs to our trip, pray give me a ſip
Of the gliſtening dew on that red pouting lip.

VIII.

With ſuch a ſweet kiſs, as that one and this,
My fortune to-day has not been ſo amiſs ;
Feel no alarm for that wound on my arm,
The ſaſh you tied over it acts like a charm ;
But fill up the cup, my Beauty, fill up,
Then, Comrades, to horſe, 'tis in France we muſt ſup.

LOVE, HONOR, AND GLORY.

I.

Like a dying old Giant the wind howled and moaned,
And ſhook with great fury the ſaſhes,
In ſadneſs of heart by the fire I groaned,
And traced out her face in the aſhes ;
The days of bright hopes like a dream had paſſed by,
And Life ſeemed a very dull ſtory,
But I thought of the time when my pulſes beat high
And I ſighed for Love, Honor, and Glory.

II.

The fire at laſt went entirely out,
And the candles, but I never miſſed them ;
For Sleep on her pinions came flying about,
And ſtooped down to my eyelids and kiſſed them ;
Forgot for the time was each fear and each doubt, —
Forgot each diſheartening ſtory, —
Forgot every grief, — and my heart became ſtout,
For I dreamed of Love, Honor, and Glory.

TO THE NIGHT WINDS.

Gentle winds, ye have come over mountain and
dale,
Ye have ſwept o'er the ocean and kiſſed the white
ſail;
Ye have entered the chamber and gazed on the
ſlumbers
Of her who is ever the theme of my numbers;
Ye have lingered awhile where my Charmer re-
poſes,
To breathe on her cheek, — that abode of the
roſes;
Ye have preſſed for a moment that delicate lip,
Where the bees of Hymettus their honey might
ſip;
Ye have hovered enraptured around her ſweet
boſom,
More fragrant than dew on the Hyacinth's bloſſom;
And as with remembrance of her ye come freighted,
My heart that was ſad becomes ſtrangely elated;
Ye can mark her repoſe in this deſolate hour,
For ye enter unheeded, where none have the power;
Then ſeek her again, in her home by the ſea,

And bear to her bedſide this meſſage from me.
Go! tell her my heart, that has loved her in gladneſs,
Would be fonder and truer in ſorrow and ſadneſs;
And through the wide world ſhe may roam nor diſ-
cover
So truthful a friend and ſo faithful a lover.
Alas, this is idle! Fate's cruel decree
Forbids that her love ſhould emparadiſe me;
But who can reſtore me my heart as ſhe found it,
Or my ſoul diſenthrall from the ſpell caſt around it?
And when the time comes that forbids all diſſem-
bling, —
When darkneſs ſurrounds, and Life's taper is trem-
bling,
I will breathe her dear name as my ſorrows are end-
ing,
And then my ſad ſoul to its Heaven aſcending
Shall bear a fond prayer to the Powers ſupernal,
That her life, like my love, may be pure and eternal.

And when o'er my aſhes the lilies are blooming,
The air that floats over me ſweetly perfuming,
Ye will pauſe by the ſpot where in peace I am lying,
Unheeding the world and its ſmiling or ſighing,
And will mark that whenever the feeling ſweeps o'er
her,
That I died, as I always had lived, her adorer,
She comes and bedews, as a ſorrowful duty,
The flowers that cannot ſurpaſs her in beauty.

STANZAS.

I.

'Tis evening, and the moon above
Doth glorioufly fhine;
And to the health of her I love
I drink this ruby wine.

II.

A thoufand leagues my heart returns,
Far, far acrofs the brine,
To her for whom my fpirit yearns,
To whom I drink this wine.

III.

Her figure, graceful as the fawn,
And flender as the vine
From which the cluftering grapes were torn
To make this glorious wine,

IV.

Would gain new ftrength, could fhe but print
Her foot befide the Rhine,

And her pale cheek would wear a tint
Tranſcending this red wine.

V.

The moon would have a ſofter charm,
A light ſtill more divine,
If ſhe were leaning on my arm
To whom I drink this wine.

VI.

If there is virtue in a prayer
That flows from lips of mine,
Her life ſhall be the Angels care,
Her happineſs divine.

A WREATH OF SMOKE.

I.

WHEN clouds, o'ercharged with care and grief,
 Seem gathering around,
'Tis in the rolled tobacco leaf
 That ſolace can be found;
With every puff there fades away
 Some true or fancied ſorrow,
And I am happy for the day,
 Whate'er betide the morrow.

II.

The graceful wreaths of ſmoke I blow,
 To yon blue Heavens aſcend,
I bleſs each one, as off they go,
 Like ſome departing friend;
And wiſh that I could ſoar above,
 Or had, like them, the power
To charm away from thoſe I love
 Each ſad and dreary hour.

ACROSS THE WAY.

I.

THE moon is ſilvering old Park-Street ſteeple,
Likewiſe the trees,
And ſleep is creeping o'er the Boſton people
By ſlow degrees.

II.

I throw my caſement open wide, and wheel
My eaſy-chair
To face the ſtreet, that I may breathe and feel
The cool night air.

III.

And while reclining here I muſe and ponder
On life's decay,
A light illuminates a chamber yonder
Acroſs the way.

IV.

And as the tongue of midnight tells the hour
From ſtreet to ſtreet,

I ſee upon the threſhold of her bower
So pure and ſweet,

V.

A Beauty ſtanding, with a form excelling
All dreams of Art,
And feel a wonderful emotion ſwelling
My throbbing heart.

VI.

How gracefully ſhe ſets the flickering candle
Upon the floor,
The while ſhe turns the little ivory handle
And bolts the door.

VII.

Then to the caſement haſtily advances
That charming maid ;
For one brief moment at the ſky ſhe glances,
Then pulls the ſhade.

VIII.

Ah ! will ſhe ſhut out this extremely fine,
Clear night of June ?
Yes ! ſhe unmaſks not beauty ſo divine
E'en to the moon.

IX.

But think not, dear, your movements are unknown,
For, by the aid
Of Fancy, and the ſhadow that is thrown
Upon the ſhade,

X.

I feel, — and either were a faithful guide, —
Extremely certain
Of all that happens on the other ſide
Of that thick curtain.

XI.

Now of your taſteful garments you're diveſting
Moſt gracefully,
To make yourſelf look ſtill more intereſting
In "*robe de nuit.*"

XII.

Acroſs the room I ſee your form ſo fair
Paſs and repaſs,
And now you're ſtanding taking down your hair
Before the glaſs.

XIII.

That hair abundant, whoſe rich golden curls
Delight beholders,

Loofed from confinement by a few quick twirls
Falls down your fhoulders, —

XIV.

Shoulders as fragrant as the airs about
The funny South, —
Now, darling, take thofe pins directly out
Of your fweet mouth.

XV.

You leave the glafs abruptly, and I find
That all is ftill ;
How fweet your pretty face muft look behind
That fnowy frill.

XVI.

And now you read a verfe of fome fweet Poet
You think divine,
Tranfported would I be, could I but know it
Were verfe of mine.

XVII.

And now upon the cufhion by the chair
Your figure bends,
And from your lips a pure and heartfelt prayer
To Heaven afcends.

XVIII.

“Nymph, in thy orisons be all my sins
Remembered” now,
And give one thought to me ere sleep begins
To touch your brow.

XIX.

So all is dark and quiet, you have just
Put out the light;
Sleep, sleep protected by the Heaven you trust!
Fair Saint, — Good night.

NEW YEAR'S EVE.

I.

Old Father Time with glaſs in hand
  And ſcythe acroſs his ſhoulder,
Is by my ſide reminding me
  That I am growing older;
And ſadly ſays the kind old man,
  In accents ſoft and clear,
"My hour-glaſs I ſoon ſhall turn,
  Then vaniſhes the year."

II.

So from this long and graceful jar
  I pour the fragrant wine,
And, when old Time turns up his glaſs,
  I'll do the ſame to mine,
And drink to all upon the land,
  And all upon the ſea,
And ſigh the while I bid Farewell
  To Eighteen Fifty-Three.

III.

I'll grieve not for deceitful friends
Whofe falfenefs I've detected,
But drink to thofe exalted hearts
I never have fufpected,
Who changing not with every turn
Of Fortune's tipfy wheel,
Are ever grappled to my foul
With hooks of triple fteel.

IV.

I'll drink to her who does not fcorn
My rude unpolifhed verfe,
Whofe love would be a talifman
Though all the world fhould curfe,
And who would fmile upon the chain
With which I'd gladly bind her, —
I'll drink to her with all my heart,
And love her, — when I find her.

MISS SWEETBRIAR'S COURTSHIP.

A BALLAD.

I.

THERE ſtood, when happened ſome ſummers ago
  The events of the following ſtory,
A large ſtone hotel, as many folks know,
  At the end of Nahant's promontory;
And when they couldn't endure the heat,
  Then all the world and its daughter,
Some of whom are "*élite*," but ſome very effete,
  Would ſtart for the ſalt ſea-water.

II.

What bevies of feminine beauties rare,
  Such as ſeen in a poet's dream are,
Going down to Nahant for the bracing air,
  Have I met in that little ſteamer;
And I thought it aware of its precious freight
  And endowed with human ſenſation,
For every plank ſeemed very elate
  And gave an extra vibration.

III.

Now of all the charmers who viſited there,
  To look at the broad Atlantic,
A few years ſince, was one who was fair,
  Surpaſſingly fair and romantic ;
But as the ſtory that I ſhall tell
  Is a very veracious hiſtory,
The name of "*la plus belle des belles*"
  Muſt remain forever a myſtery.

IV.

Yet as names are very convenient things
  To the poet who ſtrikes his lyre,
And deeds of lovers and heroes ſings,
  I ſhall call her Miſs Jane Sweetbriar ;
And this you will underſtand to be
  But a fanciful appellation,
For her real name wouldn't be breathed by me
  On any conſideration.

V.

Now Jane Sweetbriar, — with her mamma, —
  Was the very earlieſt comer,
For the rooms were engaged by her dear papa
  Throughout the entire ſummer ;
But 'twas during the month of the ſultry air,
  When the fiery dog-ſtar rages,

That occurred and tranſpired the little affair
I relate in the following pages.

VI.

Miſs Jane Sweetbriar was always told
By her mother and other relations
She was deſtined to make, in the world ſo cold,
The greateſt of all ſenſations;
That her father was wealthy, and ſhe was fair,
And by nature deſigned to wed
A reigning prince, — or the ſon and heir
Who'd be prince when his father was dead.

VII.

Now as this was inſtilled from her earlieſt youth,
Of courſe ſhe grew very inflated,
Believing it all to be goſpel truth,
And her princely lover awaited;
And though gentlemen very well born and bred,
Accompliſhed, refined, and clever,
Were attentive, ſhe bridled her haughty head
And diſtinctly ſaid, "No, Sir, never."

VIII.

Then men began to keep very aloof,
As the vulgar would ſay, "fight ſhy,"
For they never will woo when there's pretty good proof
It iſn't of uſe to try.

And I heard full many a perſon ſay,
Who of charity hadn't a particle,
That her market ſhe'd certainly overſtay
And become a ſhop-worn article.

IX.

But one Auguſt day by the boat there came,
To adorn the hotel ſociety,
A ſhort young man with a very long name
Who was dreſſed with extreme propriety,
And as he danced ſo exceedingly well,
And ſang to the ladies, divinely,
And was quite an agreeable ſea-ſhore ſwell,
He got on, of courſe, quite finely.

X.

But that he might be the better received
By the girls, he to ſome confided
That he was a Duke, which they all believed,
But I will be bleſt if I did,
For I moſt audaciouſly dared ſurmiſe
That his Grace was an impoſition,
But angry glances from beautiful eyes
Frowned on the foul ſuſpicion.

XI.

Now female artillery brought to bear,
Opened at once their fire,

And the Duke ſoon fell at the exquiſite pair
  Of feet of Miſs Jane Sweetbriar;
And Jane was as pleaſant as ſhe could be,
  And put on her airs and graces,
And it waſn't a difficult thing to ſee
  She was going through all her paces.

XII.

And if any one aſked where ſhe could be found,
  They'd ſay, "That foreigner has her,
Conſtantly walking her 'round and around
  The ladies' upper piazza."
Ah, me! If every balcony rail
  Had the means of communication,
How many a ſoft and tender tale
  It could tell of each ſweet flirtation.

XIII.

Jane's delicate blood the Duke would ſtir,
  As he'd tell, in his manner romantic,
Of the "Chateau in Spain" that was ready for her
  Juſt over the briny Atlantic.
And then he'd deſcribe the magnificent ſpot
  That was ſo like a fairy ſcene,
Juſt as mendacious Claude Melnotte
  Uſed to talk to the ſilly Pauline.

XIV.

And now one evening after tea,
  As they ſat in their room together,
Did Jane and her darling mother agree
  That the Duke had views, but whether
'Twere beſt to conſent at once, or defer,
  Was a matter for conſultation,
And mamma told Jane it was left to her,
  After ſerious converſation.

XV.

Then Jane ſaid, "Mother, I'm twenty-three,
  And no prince has come hither to wed,
And I think on the whole it were better for me
  To put up with a Duke inſtead."
And ſo 'twas decided. The following day
  The rumor abroad was carried
That Jane Sweetbriar was "*fiancée*"
  To the Duke, and would ſoon be married.

XVI.

Then how important the family grew,
  And evinced an increaſed gentility,
Which proved that they were poſſeſſing a true
  Republican love for nobility;

And even papa declared that he
  From trade would at once retire,
When on a ducal family tree
  Was engrafted a fair Sweetbriar.

XVII.

It ſoon turned out that this elegant Duke,
  (Oh, Jane, what a ſad diſaſter !)
At a New York Inn was aſſiſtant cook,
  And had robbed and fled ſrom his maſter.
Now this employed the goſſips awhile,
  And I fancied that I detected
Many a very triumphant ſmile
  On the faces of Jane's rejected.

XVIII.

To hear the remarks and perceive the ſneers
  Of her friends, was, of courſe, unpleaſant,
So ſhe went abroad to remain for years,
  And there ſhe reſides at preſent ;
And doubtleſs noblemen mark her way,
  And on Love's fleet wings purſue her,
But ſhe'll never forget till her dying day
  The counterfeit Duke, — her wooer.

TO THE BIG TREE ON BOSTON COMMON.

I.

WHEN firſt from Mother Earth you ſprung,
Ere Puritans had come among
The ſavages to looſe each tongue
In pſalms and prayers,
Theſe "Forty Acres, more or leſs,"
Now putting on their ſummer dreſs,
Were but a "howling wilderneſs"
Of wolves and bears.

II.

Moſt wondrous changes you have ſeen
Since you put forth your primal green
And tender ſhoot;
Three hundred years your life has ſpanned,
Yet calm, ſerene, erect you ſtand,
Of great renown throughout the land,
Though ſhowing marks of Time's hard hand
From crown to root.

III.

You, when a ſlender ſapling, ſaw
The perſecuted reach this ſhore
And in their turn
Treat others juſt as they'd been treated;
To mete the meaſure that's been meted,
How man does yearn.

IV.

Of tales, perchance devoid of truth,
With which they would in early youth
My heart appall,
Was one the goſſips uſed to tell
About a witch ſo grim and fell
They hung on you for raiſing — Well,
It waſn't Saul.

V.

Since you beheld the light of day
A race has nearly paſſed away, —
A warlike nation,
Who oft with fire-water plied
Loſt all their bravery and pride
And yielded to the rapid ſtride
Of annexation.

VI.

Behold, a mightier race appears
And high a vaſt Republic rears
        Her giant features,
And weſtward ſteadily we drive
The few poor Indian who ſurvive
And barely keep the race alive,—
        Degenerate creatures!

VII.

For, are we not the mighty Lords
And Maſters of all ſavage hordes
        (In our opinion)?
And when we with Inferiors deal
Do not we uſe the iron heel
And make them wince and writhe and feel
        Their Lords' dominion?

VIII.

You heard the firſt rebellious hum
Of voices, and the fife and drum
        Of revolution;
And heard the bells and welkin ring
When they threw off old George the King
And thereby gained a better thing,—
        Our Conſtitution.

IX.

And you ſtill thrive and live to ſee
The country proſperous and free,
In ſpite of all
The very ſage prognoſtications
Of prophets in exalted ſtations
Who could foretell the fate of Nations,
And ſaid ſhe'd fall.

X.

Majeſtic Tree, you've ſeen much worth
From little Boſton iſſue forth,
And many men,
Who love their kind and give their ſtore
To help the ſuffering and the Poor ; —
Heaven bleſs their wealth and grant them more,
I pray again.

XI.

And you ſhall ſee much more beſide
Ere to your root, old Boſton's pride,
The axe is laid ;
And long, I truſt, the time will be
Ere Mayor and Council ſit on thee
And find with unanimity
That you're decayed.

XII.

For you are ftill quite hale and ftanch
Though here and there perchance a branch
        Is flightly rotten,
And you will ftand and hold your fway
When he who pens this rhyme to-day
Shall mingle with the common clay
        And be forgotten.

A REVISIT.

I.

One bright and charming day laſt Fall
  Some miles of ground I wandered over
And climbed o'er many a fence and wall
  In the purſuit of quail and plover ;
But all my toil was vain and fruitleſs,
  My fowling-piece not once I fired,
The expedition proved quite bootleſs,
  And I became extremely tired.

II.

The day declined, — the Sun was ſetting,
  As is its cuſtom, in the Weſt,
And I, this world of care forgetting,
  Reclined beneath a tree to reſt ;
But ere my drowſy ſenſes failed me
  A ſtalwart farmer I deſcried,
Who from his market-wagon hailed me,
  And aſked me if I'd like to ride.

III.

"I live in Guilford, next to Stow,
  You'll fee it from the hill quite plain,
I'll drive you there and you can go
  To Bofton in the evening train."
So, thankful for the invitation
  That honeft Rufticus had offered,
I left my graffy fituation
  And took the feat fo kindly proffered.

IV.

"So, that is Guilford, — I am glad
  To fee the place; I well remember
I paffed fome months there when a lad, —
  Blefs me, the tenth of next November
Will make juft twenty years fince I
  Went there a gracelefs little fcholar
(Alas! How quickly Time flips by!)
  In corduroys and ruffled collar.

V.

"I boarded with old Parfon Short,
  Whofe dwelling ftood befide the hill."
"The Parfon's houfe I've lately bought."
  "Indeed! is he not living ftill?"

"You might have known he'd go at length
  The way of ſinner and of ſaint.
At Eighty-five he loſt his ſtrength,
  Then died, Sir, of his old complaint."

VI.

"Though croſs, he was the beſt of men,
  And I'll not let his faults outlive him,
He'll never box my ears again
  And ſo I cordially forgive him
And truſt that 'mid the ſtars and ſaints
  He now partakes celeſtial joys,
Relieved of all his bad complaints,
  The aſthma, and unruly boys.

VII.

"And where is white-haired Dr. Sloat?
  With venerable locks of ſnow;
He uſed to make my boyiſh throat
  A channel for Elixir Pro.
I think I ſee his little ſhop, —
  His bookcaſe, with its queer old fixtures
And ſtuff'd gray owl upon the top
  That ſeemed to guard the pills and mixtures.

VIII.

"The map of Europe on the wall,
  The grinning ſkull upon the ſhelf;

His patients, — did he kill them all ?"
"He did, and then he killed himſelf,
For feeling out of ſorts one day
He took his celebrated pill,
Then died, and ſince, I'm glad to ſay
We haven't had a perſon ill."

IX.

"Ah ! There's the pond I uſed to ſwim in,
And gather fragrant water-lilies
To give the ſweeteſt of young women,
Who lived near where the cider-mill is.
Yes ! ſhe my very earlieſt flame was,
(At ten Love's very hard to ſmother,)
Matilda Jane her charming name was, —
She's now a wife, I truſt, and mother."

X.

Our drives, like all drives, had an end,
We reached the parſonage at laſt ;
"Alas !" ſaid I, "my worthy friend,
This ſets me thinking of the Paſt ;
I recollect the ſpot right well,
The very woodpile ſeems the ſame ;
And there's my chamber in the L,
To which no ſunbeams ever came.

XI.

" The venerable tree that bore
  Thoſe pears ſo puckery and hard,
Is ſtanding, as it did of yore,
  Right in the middle of the yard ;
And there's the church, — I ſee the vane
  Is pointing ſtill to ſou'-ſou'-weſt ;
It always did, — but why complain
  Of aught that does its very beſt ? "

XII.

I'll take a ſeat on yonder wall
  The while I'm waiting for the train,
My bygone joys and griefs recall,
  And live my boyhood o'er again ;
But ſtay ! if life I've found is not
  Juſt what my youthful fancy painted,
And I reviſit this old ſpot
  With care and ſorrow well acquainted,

XIII.

And if no gentle heart is near me,
  Beating reſponſive to my own,
To aid, to counſel, and to cheer me,
  But I Life's battle fight alone ;
Why ſhould I rend the veil apart
  That keeps the Paſt from coming o'er me,

6

To caſt a ſhadow on my heart,
  When I've the Future all before me?"

XIV.

There ſtill are prizes worth the ſtrife,
  And Fame and Honor to the gainer;
The ſoul that takes ſad views of life
  Should let this wholeſome truth ſuſtain her;
My heart, leſs buoyant than of yore,
  Still aſks of Fortune proſperous breezes,
I've puſhed my ſhallop from the ſhore,
  Its fate to be what Heaven pleaſes.

TO A CLASSMATE.

"We have heard the chimes at midnight."

HENRY IV., SECOND PART.

I.

OLD times come o'er me, and I fain would hear
Something of one my heart holds ever dear, —
Whether he's living;
Oh, can it be that he I love has gone
Whence there is no return, to that long bourn?
I've my misgiving.

II.

So now, my friend, for want of something better,
I'll send this very short and rhyming letter,
To ascertain
If you still live, and recollect the chimes
We've heard at midnight. Those delightful times
Come not again!

III.

And how ofttimes to Fancy's realms we'd mount,
And drink deep draughts — from the Pierian fount,
To banish cares;

Then bivalve broils that marred the night's repofe,
And then the larks, — I mean with which we rofe
In time for prayers !

IV.

Our clafs is fcattered. Some by trade have thriven
And fome have laid their treafure up in heaven,
(A fafe inveftment,)
And there are fome the young idea who teach,
And fome who practife, fome who only preach,
But here's no jeft meant.

V.

Some live in town, their quiet way purfuing,
Who would be pleafed to hear what you are doing,
And how you are ;
So write us word, in profe, or woo the Mufe ;
That you do either well, whene'er you choofe,
We're quite aware.

VI.

How are your talents ? Have they run to wafte ?
Do you ftill write, or have you loft your tafte
For the poetic ?
Are you religious ? Have you joined the church ?
And have you found, or are you ftill in fearch
Of the Æfthetic ?

VII.

Do you find aught that gives you ſatisfaction ?
Does life preſent to you the ſame attraction
It did "lang ſyne ?"
Or have your hopes of winning fame and glory,
And being widely known, in ſong and ſtory
Vaniſhed, like mine ?

VIII.

Unleſs you've ſadly changed, I know you've gained
The peace that's purchaſed by a life unſtained,
Upright and moral ;
More ſatisfactory than vulgar praiſe,
And better, nobler far, than poets' bays,
Or heroes' laurel.

IX.

Write me and tell me how you paſs the time,
In your delightful and far-diſtant clime
Of fruits and flowers.
But ere I cloſe, perhaps you'd like to know
Of ſome with whom you paſſed, a while ago,
Such pleaſant hours.

X.

Well ; Kate ſtill plays her tinkling guitar,
And ſits and gazes at that favorite ſtar
She named for you,

And ſighs and languiſhes, and rolls her eye ;
She thinks you're coming back ! (At one time I
Believed that true.)

XI.

And as for Caroline, ſhe took offence,
Merely becauſe I ſaid ſhe wanted ſenſe !
So we don't ſpeak.
Poor little Sue, with whom you uſed to ride,
Laſt June was married ; and the darling died
Within a week !

XII.

How could you find it in your heart to leave her !
She was a ſplendid girl ; in fact, I never
Have ſeen a finer.
Her ſiſter Jane — whom, doubtleſs, you remember —
Married a miſſionary, laſt November,
And went to China.

XIII.

And now, farewell ! — my horſe is at the door ;
I'm for a ride, and therefore can't ſay more.
I really miſs you,
And mean to write again, ſome future day,
But now I've merely time enough to ſay,
God bleſs you.

A COURSE OF BARK.

Of Peter Van Duyſen, a Dutchman by birth,
But a toper by habit and tanner by trade,
Who for many a year but encumbered the earth,
Yet at laſt of the Church was an ornament made,
Whoſe true reformation
And regeneration
So ſtruck with ſurpriſe every friend and relation,
Aſtoniſhed his neighbors, delighted his wife,
(Who had long felt aggrieved by his diſſolute life):
And the cauſe of his ſudden return to the fold,
Of which the particulars never were told,
And have hitherto been ſo enveloped in myſtery,
The beneficent muſe
Will no longer refuſe
To relate the authentic and wonderful hiſtory.

Now, Peter perceived not the ſhame and diſgrace
Of a thickneſs of ſpeech and a rubicund face,
And the name he had gained of "a very hard caſe;"
And the deeper he drank
The more deeply he ſank,
Till his body was nought but an alcohol tank.

The day had long paſſed ſince he offered his reaſons
For conſtant libations, at all times and ſeaſons ;
And though ſuch apologies ſeldom are ſound,
Nor ſupported by reaſoning very profound,
Yet I never would ſneer at them,
Laugh at or jeer at them,
Or hurl an expreſſion uncommonly queer at them,
For they prove that their maker is fully awake
To the fact that he runs 'gainſt the views of ſoci-
ety,
And feels himſelf called on excuſes to make,
Juſt to ſhow he's not loſt to all ſenſe of propri-
ety.
Mr. A. takes a drop for a pain in his head,
And he thinks it will cure him without any queſ-
tion ;
Mr. B. drinks becauſe he has oft heard it ſaid
A little good brandy aſſiſts the digeſtion ;
Mr. C. will remark he's been ill for a week ;
Mr. D. has a very bad pain in his cheek ;
Mr. E. fears the ſalad may poſſibly hurt him ;
Mr. F. has the blues, and he drinks to divert him ;
The powerful argument offered by G.,
Is that, much to his joy, he has lately been told
Hot whiſky and water is good for a cold ;
And ſo it goes on down to X., Y., and Z.
The reaſons for what a man wiſhes to do,
Though oftentimes weak, yet are never a few.

I once knew a man ſo addicted to grog
That he'd drink till his ſenſes were loſt in a fog,
Becauſe he'd been working, he ſaid, like a dog.
I preſume that the meaning he wiſhed to convey
Was, of courſe, that he'd been working hard all the
day;
But, as far as my own ſmall experience goes,
The work that all thoſe that belong to the race
Called canine, perform, is, in ſome ſunny place,
(Forever preferring the large cellar-doors,)
With their jaws ſoftly cuſhioned on both their fore-
paws,
To ſniff off the flies as they light on their noſe,—
And I always opined
He was that way inclined,
For, though earneſtly ſeeking, I never could find,
That ſcience or art or religion or trade
Had ever derived the leaſt poſſible aid
From any exertion he ever had made.

Now, I advocate always exceſſive ſobriety,
Though I never have joined a tee-total ſociety,
And might not ſay nay,
On a very hot day,
To a very large goblet of champagne "*frappé*,"
Regardleſs of all Mrs. Grundy might ſay,
And provided, of courſe, there was nothing to pay;
Yet, 'tis better to keep from temptation away,

For I learned when a lad, in a ſchool of deſign,
What a very hard matter is *drawing a line.*

But it ſeems, while I pen this irregular metre,
That I'm ſaying uncommonly little of Peter.
So, without more ado, I will briefly relate
His narrow eſcape from a danger he ran,
By which he was ſaved from a terrible fate,
And inſtantly made a reſpectable man.

Though Peter, I've ſaid, was a tanner by trade,
Yet a fortune by tanning he never had made,—
For buſineſs of any kind needs attention,
A fact it is never amiſs to mention,—
And his cuſtomers fled from him, one after one,
When they found that his work was moſt wretchedly done,
And ſaw what a rig he was trying to run.
Then he'd nothing to do, yet for ſpirits he'd ſpend,
And ſoon diſcovered, with many regrets,
That *liquor* will never *liqui*-date debts,
And his courſe muſt ſpeedily come to an end.
His creditors clamored for their demands,
And his tannery ſoon paſſed out of his hands;
With the brindle dog he was forced to part,
Which touched, though it didn't renew, his heart.
His wife worked on in grief and pain,
That her child ſhouldn't cry for bread in vain;

And ſhe ſtruggled and hoped, as women will,
While Peter ſank lower and lower ſtill ;
  Soliciting alms of each paſſer-by,
Drinking throughout the day his fill,
  And lodging at night in the neareſt ſty.
If I picture him truly, you'll ſay I draw
As wretched a being as ever you ſaw.
But ſtill, in the midſt of his downward courſe,
Would ariſe a feeling of deep remorſe,
That would lead him oft in ſorrow at night —
  When ghoſts and goblins gibber and moan,
Who are never beheld by the morning light —
  To viſit the tannery once his own ;
And one ſtormy night, as he ſtaggered along,
Meandering the hides and the vats among,
While the wind blew high and the night was dark,
  There came a guſt that took off his hat ;
He tried to catch it, but reeled and fell,
And down he went with a fearful yell,
  Tumbling headlong into a vat,
There to go through with *a courſe of bark.*

Down he went, and he ſplaſhed and ſpluttered,
And fierce were the cries that the victim uttered ;
But fruitleſs all, — there was no one near, —
Not a human being with ears to hear,
And a heart to feel, and a rope to throw ;
  Yet, had there been, I can ſcarcely tell,

(For what others will do no one can know,)
  If they wouldn't have thought it juſt as well,
And have left him to tan with the hides below.

Then Peter's agony ſoon began,
  For his paſt career appeared before him,
And he knew himſelf a deteſted man,
  And that none would in the leaſt deplore him ;
He knew repentance was all too late,
That he ſoon muſt yield to impending fate,
Down, down to ſink, and there to ſtay,
Till ſome, Heaven knows how diſtant, day,
When they'd find him tanned in the uſual way ;
Then how they'd laugh, and ſpeculate whether
He'd make on the whole a durable leather,
And load him with well-deſerved abuſe,
And ſay that for once they'd make him of uſe,
And then into ſoles they'd cut up his body,
So well preſerved by the tan and the toddy.

But while this ruſhed acroſs his brain,
He twice went down and roſe again ;
And now his ſtrength was failing faſt,
  And weaker grew each vain endeavor —
One bubbling ſhriek — it was the laſt
  Of Peter, who then ſank forever, —
Or would, had not that deathly cry
Struck on the ear of a paſſer-by,

In the ſhape of the ſame intelligent brute
  That Peter had owned in his beſt eſtate ;
And now of his kindneſs he reaped the fruit,
  By being ſaved from a fearful fate ;
For this moſt grateful of brindled Towzers,
      With a bound, and a daſh,
      And a howl, and a ſplaſh,
Jumped into the vat, as quick as a flaſh,
And faſtened his jaws in a leg of his trowſers.

Ah ! how one's experience conſtantly teaches
What many a ſtern and cold moraliſt preaches,
That Gilead poſſeſſes for all men a balm,
And a ſtorm is a certain forerunner of calm,
      And when all things appear
      Moſt dark, cheerleſs, and drear,
That circumſtance proves that the daylight is near ;
For, when grief and deſpondency wholly enſlave us,
  And ſad the forebodings and fears of the heart,
When it ſeems as if nought from deſtruction could ſave us,
  And the laſt rays of hope in the darkneſs depart,
Unlooked-for aſſiſtance will raiſe and aſſuage us,
Although adventitious, yet moſt advantageous.

But the courſe of events to delay by reflections,
In a writer of tales, is the worſt of objections ;
And I think I ſhall run little hazard in ſtating,

That when ſuch a perſon abandons narrating,
And takes in its ſtead both to proſing and prating,
He's a bore of a ſize that there's no overrating;
And one's hero to leave at a critical time
Should be reckoned by readers not leſs than a crime;
And I ought to have ſaid
That Peter, half-dead,
Was reſcued when hope had entirely fled,
And have told you at once how his canine preſerver,
By tugging with *dog*-gedneſs, vigor, and fervor,
Through the darkneſs a guide,
Brought him cloſe to the ſide
Of the vat, where a rope had been recently tied.
If a man when he's drowning will catch at a ſtraw,
Why, of courſe, he will catch at a rope all the more;
So Peter ſtruck out, and at laſt made a graſp
At the rope, and held on with the muſcular claſp
Of a man who is juſt at his very laſt gaſp;
And there he hung for the reſt of the night,
Till the morning broke with its ſtreaks of light,
When ſeveral workmen, who happened to paſs,
Saved both of the brutes from their perilous ſtate,
And they carried Peter right out of the gate,
Acroſs the road to a field of graſs,
And there they punched him, and rolled him over;
And you'll not deny when I venture to ſtate
That, though in the graſs, yet he waſn't in clover;
But ſucceſs attended the operation,

And reſtored the ſuſpended animation,
By bringing on the proper pulſation ;
And he came to himſelf, and then went to his wife,
A different man for the reſt of his life.

No muſe of mine poſſeſſes the art
  To tell in any poetical ſtrain
Of the rapture pervading a woman's heart,
Whatever her rank and worldly ſtation,
  When ſhe finds that her prayers were not made in vain,
  For of joy that ſeems a foretaſte of Heaven
  A true portrayal can never be given,
But muſt ever be left to imagination.

I fear I'm tedious, ſo I'll briefly ſay,
That Peter lived from that eventful day —
  Or night — an honeſt, prudent, upright man ;
And many a long-loſt friend of old
Held forth his hand when he was told,
  That for the future Peter had a plan.
By toil and prudence, and ſome ſlight aſſiſtance,
  He, ſtep by ſtep, regained the ground he'd loſt.
To all temptation he made fierce reſiſtance,
  Thinking experience was not worth its coſt.
Now firſt at meeting, loudeſt in the prayer,
  You'd ſcarce ſuppoſe he'd e'er from virtue drifted ;

And many a perſon I have heard declare,
  That in exhorting he ſeemed truly gifted.
Soon fortune ſmiled, for vice was at an end,
  And though 'twas humble, he adorned his ſtation ;
To all good projects was a zealous friend,
  And gave his ſon a liberal education ;
And oft in after years, when old and fat,
  The village boys at eve would cluſter round him,
To hear him tell the ſtory of the Vat,
  And how poor dead and buried Towzer found him.
Perchance the precepts that he threw around
Did not fall profitleſs on barren ground.

TO THE MERMAID.

> "Thou comeſt in ſuch a queſtionable ſhape
> That I will ſpeak to thee."
>
> HAMLET.

I.

Mysterious Hybrid! Near the Fejee Iſles
You were entrapped, they ſay, one Summer's eve,
When, unſuſpicious of the ſeaman's wiles,
You ſweetly ſung, (but this I can't believe,)
With execution that outrivalled Grisi,
Arias from operas by no means eaſy.

II.

Strange denizen of ſomewhere in the deep,
You come to us ſo very well preſerved
That we might think you in the tranquil ſleep
Your innocence and beauty well deſerved,
Although your graceful figure's quite erect;
For what from Mermaids could we not expect?

III.

But there's no power now in your dark eyes
To look with ſcorn upon the dandy's ſuit,

You anſwer not to beauty's ſmiles and ſighs ;
  Then muſt that heart be ſtilled, that tongue be mute ;
And this glaſs caſe, excluding you from air,
Proves the ſad fact that life is abſent there.

IV.

I promiſed me a very pleaſant taſk,
  And hoped to paſs the evening *tête-â-tête ;*
There's many a queſtion that I wiſhed to aſk,
  Concerning all the cuſtoms of your ſtate ;
I'm getting up a book, and looked to you
For ſtores of information ſtrange and new.

V.

I wiſhed to know if Mermaids had a king,
  Or choſe a preſident each year or two, —
Had ſtringent laws, for that's the ſort of thing
  To make the populace their duty do ;
Or lived together in a crazed community,
Where each did as he liſted, with impunity ;

VI.

And all that happens in thoſe coral groves
  That you inhabit in the realms below ;
If you write tender verſes to your loves,
  If there's a place where naughty Mermaids go, —

If you have lectures in the Winter feafon, —
And if your Poets write both rhyme and reafon?

VII.

If you have Mermaid lawyers and divines,
  And if the laft fay everything is vanity;
Whether you fpeculate in copper mines,
  And are not Mermaids fubject to infanity;
If pure falt water's all you have to drink,
And if your tails don't fometimes get a kink?

VIII.

Fond of the water you muft furely be,
  But do you have regattas every year?
And do you navigate the briny fea
  In fea-weed barks, — or ufe your tails to fteer
Some fcooped-out tortoife fhells from grot to grot;
And is there any one who owns a yacht?

IX.

Are any of the Mermaids politicians?
  Do they fulfil each promife to the letter?
And do you find, if you employ phyficians,
  That of their ftuff the lefs you take the better
Your health becomes? In fact, I'm very fure
You muft be patrons of the "Water Cure."

X.

Do you prohibit ſmoking in the ſtreets?
  Do you confine the voting to the males?
What is the ſalutation when one meets
  Another Mermaid? Do you ſhake your tails?
Is charity much practiſed in the ſea,
Or do you fancy ſcandal with your tea?

XI.

Have you the Magazines and the Reviews?
  Do any of your ſpinſters have the vapors?
How ſoon do you obtain the ſteamer's news?
  And pray, do all the Mermaids take the papers?
Do your young men do military duty?
And what's the ſtandard market-price of putty?

XII.

But this is uſeleſs, — the grim tyrant, Death,
  Has placed his icy hand upon your brow;
Had I been near, to catch your parting breath,
  (It's very ſafe for me to ſay ſo, now,)
I might have gained a maſs of information
That now is loſt to me and to the nation.

XIII.

I grieve to think ſome infidels there be
  Who ſmile in ſcorn whene'er your name they hear,

Make it a point to difbelieve in thee,
And dare to fpeak with fupercilious fneer,
Who fay you are a wondrous incongruity,
A fpecimen of Yankee ingenuity.

XIV.

As for myfelf, I'm willing to believe
In all that travellers delight to tell;
I think the mefmerizers don't deceive,
I frown on thofe who fay that you're a "fell;"
I think all the magicians fuperhuman,
And will believe the Giantefs a woman.

XV.

I place a truft in the Aërial Ship,
My love for the Hydrarchos is quite fervent,
I've cruifed about our coaft to get a peep
At my much flighted friend, the great Sea Serpent.
A man can't put himfelf to nobler ufes
Than taking fides with thofe the world abufes.

XVI.

And now, farewell! There's more that I could fay,
For my regard becomes each moment ftronger,
But I'll poftpone it for fome other day;
This won't be read, if it is any longer;
You'll triumph yet, defpite the fceptic's laugh,
Marvellous fpecimen of half and half!

A NIGHT IN THE RURAL DISTRICTS.

HOW THE WRITER PLAYED THE FRIEND OF HUMANITY, — THE RESULT OF THE SAME, AND AN INSTRUCTIVE MORAL DEDUCED THEREFROM.

It was a drear December night,
My duties were performed, —
The Chairman, as he paid my fee,
Remarked how hard it ſtormed ;
Perhaps he thought the lecture poor —
Or, didn't think at all,
Or didn't care what might that night
The lecturer befall ;
I aſked him where the Tavern was, —
He pointed down the ſtreet,
So Tavernward I bent my ſteps
And faced the cutting ſleet.
"What ho, within there, Houſe ! I ſay !
Oh, bleſs your ſcraggy head !
Grim Boniface, and give to me
This ſtormy night a bed ! "
He faintly ſmiled and ſaid to me
He'd do the beſt he could,

While I, as faintly ſmiling back,
  Replied, I hoped he would.
"I think," ſaid he, "I have a room
  That has a bed to ſpare;"
"Enough," ſaid I, "my wearied frame
  Is anxious to be there."
He led the way, — I followed him
  To — I forget the number;
Two beds were there, in one I ſaw
  A traveller in ſlumber.
Five minutes later, and diſrobed
  And gazing at the ceiling,
I felt the charms of drowſineſs
  O'er all my ſenſes ſtealing;
But when "the early village" clock
  Announced that it was four,
I was awakened by a yawn
  That ſounded like a roar,
I ſlily caſt my eyes about
  And ſaw my unknown friend
In very ſlim apparel, and
  A-ſitting up on end;
He rubbed his eyes, he ſcratched his noſe,
  He liſtened to the ſtorm,
His teeth they chattered in his head
  As if he waſn't warm;
And while I lay and looked at him,
  I wondered more and more,

And ſaw him glance towards my bed
  And ſtep upon the floor,
Then hurry on his clothes and tie
  His tippet round his throat,
And put his head inſide his hat
  And button up his coat,
Then walk up to the glaſs and take
  His razor in his hand, —
The while on every pore of mine
  Did watery globules ſtand;
I thought he meant to kill me, and
  Made ready for a ſpring,
But it ſeems he waſn't thinking
  Of any ſuch a thing,
For he put it in his carpet-bag
  And ſlowly turned the key,
And as he drew it from the lock
  He looked again at me;
And then the ſole hypotheſis
  By which theſe movements myſtic
I could explain, was that the man
  Had turns ſomnambuliſtic.
My kindly feelings roſe at this, —
  Thought I, this luckleſs ſtranger
I muſt obſerve, to ſee that he
  Comes not to any danger;
He took his carpet-bag and left
  And ſoftly cloſed the door, —

One inftant, and I ftood erect
  In middle of the floor,
Then dreffed myfelf with greater fpeed
  Than ever yet did mortal,
And feized my hat, crept down the ftairs,
  And iffued from the portal;
I faw him crofs a turnip-field
  And then the turnpike take,
And as I thought he was *afleep*,
  I followed in his *wake;*
I wondered where he meant to go,
  And fancied, with a fhiver,
His object was to drown himfelf
  On coming to the river;
But no; he fafely croffed the bridge,
  While I crept clofe behind,
Prepared to feize him if he feemed
  To fuicide inclined;
He then pufhed on to where there ftood
  A little way-fide inn,
And there he knocked until he woke
  The bar-keeper within;
I, looking through the window-panes,
  Diftinctly faw him take
A glafs of fomething hot and ftrong
  As if he were awake;
Then out he came and on he fped,
  In feeming defperation,

For three long miles until he reached
  A lonesome railway station ;
The truth flashed out, — he meant to throw
  Himself across the track,
And so Humanity forbade
  My longer holding back,
And as the day was breaking fast
  I felt a trifle bolder,
So walked up to the wretched man
  And slapped him on the shoulder ;
He turned on me most tiger-like
  And said, "Confound your eyes !
Just you be careful how you take
  A fellow by surprise."
I stammered out — because the case
  Admitted no dissembling —
That I had followed him for miles
  With all my members trembling,
For fear lest into danger's jaws
  He might perchance be brought
While he was walking in his sleep,
  As I sincerely thought.
He looked at me from head to foot,
  Then sneeringly he said,
"You're either drunk or cracked or else
  The fools are not all dead."
And thus for merely yielding to
  The dictates of humanity,

I was accuſed of drunkenneſs,
Of folly, and inſanity ;
A leſſon then and there was taught,—
To mind my own affairs,
And in ſpite of all temptation,
To let other folks mind theirs.

TO A BUTTERFLY AT SEA.

I.

'Tis very kind, though vaſtly queer,
That you ſhould call to ſee me here,
And I'll addreſs you;
For though I cannot underſtand
How you came out ſo far from land,
And you'll not tell, yet there's my hand,
I greet and bleſs you!

II.

But ſhould as ſoon expect to ſee
Moſs-roſe-buds on the main croſſ-tree;
(Ah, how I'd pet them!)
Or 'round about the capſtan's foot
A bed of violets taking root,
And telling me, although they're mute,
Not to forget them! —

III.

Or in the ſhadow of the ſail
A lily lifting up her pale
And lovely face,

As on the ratlines to eſpy
A gay and brilliant butterfly,
Seeking in vain, with anxious eye,
One flowery place.

IV.

Sail on with us, — there's no objection,
And you can truſt in my protection,
For you're to me
Suggeſtive of green fields and flowers,
Woodbine and honeyſuckle bowers,
And call to mind delightful hours,
Of which, when ſadneſs overpowers,
I think at ſea.

V.

The pantry-door ſhall ne'er be cloſed,
And not a wiſh ſhall be oppoſed,
If you'll remain.
The ſugar-bowl ſhall yield its ſweets,
We'll give you ſome luxurious treats,
And ope our many potted meats,
And beſt champagne.

VI.

Go, range the cabin through and through,
And truſt me when I ſwear to you,
As I'm a ſinner,

That, ſhould the ſteward thwart your wiſhes,
I'll break his head with his own diſhes,
And hurl his carcaſs to the fiſhes,
For dinner.

VII.

You heed me not; and now you're gone,
To tempt the mighty deep alone
And unprotected.
No! One who hears the raven's cry,
And marks each ſparrow fall and die,
Watches o'er all with ſleepleſs eye
And even a ſimple butterfly
Is not neglected.

VIII.

And he the rhymeſter, who to-day
Has wooed you in an idle lay,
Is but like you
A wanderer acroſs the ſeas,
And dreams away theſe days of eaſe,
Entranced with idle fantaſies,
Sweet, though untrue.

IX.

And though to ſerious contemplation,
And calm and pious meditation,
Too oft a ſtranger,

Knows that the ſtrong, protecting arm,
That can ſubdue the fierceſt ſtorm,
Is thrown around his powerleſs form,
In time of danger.

AN ANSWER TO AN INVITATION TO DINE

——————— "cui corpus porrigitur."
VIRGIL.

I.

I'VE juſt received your invitation
  To a rare banquet, thus you 'clept it,
And much regret my ſituation
  Is ſuch that I cannot accept it;
No dining out is there for me now,
  My illneſs is ſufficient reaſon;
And could you but look in you'd ſee now
  That I am laid up for a ſeaſon.

II.

In payment for my ſins I've caught a
  Diſtreſſing cold, and am in bed,
With napkins wet with rum and water
  Twiſted around my aching head.
It ſeems as if that nameleſs Gent.,
  With cloven foot and ſable coat,
On my annihilation bent,
  Had fixed his talons in my throat.

III.

My voice, whoſe tones, if not o'er pleaſant,
Would doubtleſs very much delight you,
Is ſilent, and if you were preſent,
I could not ſay what now I write you.
You'll find it not an eaſy taſk
Deciphering this wretched ſcrawl,
But he can ſome indulgence aſk
Who writes in bed againſt the wall.

IV.

So when you read this lucubration,
I muſt requeſt you'll not be critical;
Conſider that my ſituation
Is not by any means poetical.
A bliſter that could draw a wagon
Uſurps poſſeſſion of my cheſt;
It ſeems as if a fiery dragon
Had made his home upon my breaſt.

V.

I'm being now, like gold, refined
With very fierce and raging fires,
But not exactly of the kind
That wit or verſe-making inſpires.
With not a thing to eat or drink,
One can't be very bright or merry,

I'd feel much better now, I think,
  If I could have a glaſs of Sherry.

VI.

I'll own the wine-cup I have drained
  Since I've been ſtretched upon my back,
But then the wine the cup contained
  Is known as Wine of Ipecac ;
And that, my candid mind confeſſes,
  (A fact I feel convinced that you know,)
Does not alleviate diſtreſſes
  As much as your delicious "Juno."

VII.

Juſt as the clock is ſtriking five
  I'll know you're ſitting down to dinner,
And at that time, if I'm alive,
  I'll pledge you in a draught of Senna ;
And ſigh to loſe thoſe ſcintillations
  From wit that never yet was ſpiteful,
And all your brilliant coruſcations
  Of fancy that are ſo delightful.

VIII.

Pleaſe give your gueſts to underſtand
  I'd gladly meet them at that hour,
Were not misfortune's heavy hand
  Upon me with reſiſtleſs power ;

And though "*in propria perſona*"
  To viſit them I'll not be able,
My ſpirit yet may have the honor
  To come and rap upon the table.

IX.

When riſing from the board the crowd are
  "*Vino ciboque*" quite "*gravatus*,"
I ſhall be taking Dover's powder
  And mourning my unhappy "*ſtatus*."
Then let me hope they'll kindly think
  Of him who pens this trifling ſtanza,
And filling up their glaſſes, drink
  Confuſion to the Influenza!

A CHARCOAL SKETCH.

"Perhaps, and then again perhaps not."
Familiar Saying.

I MEET a fellow often in my way,
Urging a horſe and wagon through the ſtreets,
And ſhouting "Charcoal!" to each one he meets;
I paſſed him in the thoroughfare to-day
But did not ridicule his features grim,—
His ragged coat, and hat without a brim.
Thought I, "That fellow in thoſe ſhabby clothes,
Driving all day his ſhapeleſs horſe and cart,
Owes nothing to the tailor or his art,
Like many of our gallant city beaux;
And would that all of us, like him, could ſay,
Each night, that our purſuits throughout the day
Had left no tarniſh harder to eraſe
Than what he has upon his hands and face!
There's not a ſpot of black upon his heart,
It's all upon his face and hands and cart,

And he may ſtand a better chance to go
To Heaven than I, or many that I know."

But this was Fancy's work, and we,
Though better dreſſed, perchance, are juſt as good
as he.

THE JILTED KNIGHT.

A BALLAD.

I.

A GALLANT knight and lady bright,
(They termed them thus of yore,)
Beneath a tree, love, conſtancy,
And truth forever ſwore.

II.

"My deareſt love! the Heavens above
Record the vows we've made;
With many a knight I go to fight
Upon a great cruſade;

III.

'Tis honor calls me from my halls
And far, my love, from thee,
With my good ſword, from Paynim horde
The Holy Land to free.

IV.

It rends my heart ſrom thee to part,
  But love muſt yield to duty;
For valor, Fame ſhall ſpread my name
  As far as thine for beauty.

V.

And though, alas! a twelvemonth paſs,
  My truth is pledged forever, —
You'll not forget our ſouls have met?"
  The lady anſwered, "Never."

VI.

One long, laſt ſip of her ſweet lip —
  One preſſure of the hand —
The knight beſtrode his ſteed and rode
  Towards the Holy Land.

VII.

The lady ſighed and ſobbed and cried
  To ſee him ride away;
In wretched plight ſhe paſſed that night
  And part of the next day.

VIII.

But ere the ſun its courſe had run
  Another knight came by, —

She ſmoothed each treſs, arranged her dreſs,
  And wiped her tearful eye.

IX.

This knight he ſwore, though ne'er before
  He'd ſet his eyes upon her,
That he'd prefer to live for her
  Than die for empty honor.

X.

She ceaſed her ſighs, and raiſed her eyes
  That late with tears had gliſtened,
And could but hear thoſe vows ſincere, —
  Becauſe in ſooth ſhe liſtened.

XI.

Perchance ſhe thought, as life was ſhort,
  One lover near at hand
Was worth at leaſt ten in the Eaſt, —
  Far in the Holy Land.

XII.

For juſt ſuppoſe that Paynim foes
  Should ſlay that abſent lover, —
Slight good 'twould do that ſhe'd been true,
  When Love's ſweet dream was over.

XIII.

As years advance, lefs grows their chance
  To captivate mankind :
This fact, they fay, will often fway
  A lovely woman's mind.

XIV.

A bitter truth it is, that youth
  And beauty do not tarry,
So ere they go, all maidens know
  'Tis better that they marry.

XV.

One ne'er would end did he pretend
  To ftate how fome will ufe
Pure logic's art, their want of heart
  And falfenefs to excufe.

XVI.

O'er meadow, dale, and hill and vale
  The bridal bells rang out,
While one true knight in bloody fight
  Was putting fcores to rout.

XVII.

'Neath burning fun brave deeds were done,
  Through love of her and glory, —

That her dear name by his great fame
  Might live in ſong and ſtory.

XVIII.

Her ſcarf he wore his breaſt before,—
  Upon his helm her glove,—
Some Poet ſings, what fooliſh things
  Wiſe men will do for love.

XIX.

Where lances gleamed and banners ſtreamed
  And life-blood ebbed away,
Oh, would that knight had loſt the fight
  And fallen in the fray!

XX.

Thrice happy he right peacefully
  To ſleep among the dead,
Than live to find in womankind
  His faith forever fled.

MORAL.

XXI.

Now ſhould you be by Love's decree
  Poſſeſſor of a treaſure,
Whoſe loſs would make you loth to take
  In life the ſlighteſt pleaſure,

XXII.

There's one great rule, and he's a fool
  Whoever dares difcard it: —
Go not afar to fcenes of war,
  But ftay at home and guard it.

XXIII.

Scorn confidence, — let common fenfe
  Alone be your advifer,
Or elfe fome morn you'll wake forlorn,
  A fadder man, and wifer.

ROMEO MONTAGUE TO JULIET CAPULET.

I.

DEAR JULIET, come down from your lattice ſo high,
I've no ladder with which I can reach you;
There's no dew on the graſs and the walks are quite dry,
So, deareſt, deſcend, I beſeech you!
Love-making you'll find very nice, if you'll try,
And I'm juſt the perſon to teach you.

II.

I have come over roads very ſtony and rough,
And through perils ſevere that beſet me,
Nor tarried to aſk of each Capulet gruff
If to love you he's willing to let me;
I'd have proved myſelf made of moſt obſtinate ſtuff
To each and to all, had they met me.

III.

At a very great riſk to my clothes and my neck,
I have clambered right over the wall,
And the broken glaſs-bottles its ſummit that deck
Did not ſcare or reſtrain me at all, —

Though I knew I would be a moſt terrible wreck,
If by chance I ſhould happen to fall.

IV.

Nor fear I the ſword of your big, burly brother,
Who, perhaps, now is hovering nigh,
But I'll dare every danger each night for another
Bright glance from your dark rolling eye.
It's no eaſy thing, let me tell you, to ſmother
The flame that is lighted on high!

V.

He who ne'er has been wounded may well jeſt at ſcars,
And to overcome peril eſſay,
Broken bottles ſet endwiſe, nor locks, bolts, and bars,
Can keep a true lover away;
Then by the ſoft light of the innocent ſtars,
Liſt to all the ſweet things I've to ſay.

VI.

It ſeems you object to my family name,—
I would I'd my viſiting card;
For although for my name 'tis not I who's to blame,
Yet I'd tear in ten pieces the word;
But for ſuch a ſlight cauſe to extinguiſh Love's flame
Would truly be vaſtly abſurd.

VII.

The flower we fancy ſo much as a roſe
Would aſſuredly ſeem juſt as ſweet,
And be as agreeable to eyes and to noſe
If we called it a carrot or beet,
And I as John Smith or Tom Brown, I ſuppoſe,
Would appear juſt as well in the ſtreet.

VIII.

So in order no more to be under a ban,
And denied an acceſs to your door,
I'll have my name changed juſt as ſoon as I can,
Nor be Romeo Montague more;
To think aught a ſacrifice — I'm not the man —
That is done for the girl I adore.

IX.

Then, Juliet, deſcend from that balcony high,
I've a ſermon on Love that I'll preach you, —
We'll take a nice walk 'round the garden ſo dry,
So, deareſt, come down, I beſeech you;
Love-making, I think, you will like if you try,
And I know 'twill be pleaſant to teach you.

THE REASON WHY.

I.

Her eye was like the violet
 When morning dews are on it,
Her cheek competed with the roſe
 She wore in her Spring bonnet,
Her lips were cherries in the ſun
 Juſt ripening on the ſtem,
Her teeth were like the gliſtening pearls
 On royal diadem.

II.

Her figure was ſuperb, — her grace
 Seemed really ſuperhuman,
For Nature ſometimes does her beſt
 To beautify a Woman ;
In ſooth ſhe was a lovely thing
 For Memory to recall,
And yet he wooed her not — becauſe
 Her dividends were ſmall.

TO MY UMBRELLA.

I.

My well-tried friend, we've been together
Through many a change of wind and weather
Three years and more ;
While ſtrolling down the London Strand,
To satisfy a ſhower's demand
And ſave my clothes, I made a ſtand
At what appeared a " Hat, cap, and
Umbrella ſtore."

II.

And then and there I purchaſed you,
The beſt of all that were on view,
For one pound one,
And never ſince have felt regret
For what I paid ; you're worth it yet,
And I confeſs that getting wet
Affords no fun.

III.

While looking at you through the ſmoke
(That now enſhrouds me like a cloak)
Of my cigar,

My Fancy, for the humor's ſake,
A backward range eſſays to take,
And ſpeak of what has helped to make
You what you are.

IV.

Some tree that raiſed its branches high
As if to paint the azure ſky,
Was forced to fall,
And from a portion of its wood,
Your ſtaff was made, ſo ſtrong and good
That many a fearſul gale has ſtood
Nor cracked at all.

V.

From the deep boſom of the earth,
Where they experience quite a dearth
Of light and air,
The miner with his pick and ſpade,
Has dug the ore from which were made
The tips you wear.

VI.

A monſter who affects the ſea
Has been prevailed upon to be
Harpooned 'till dead.
And from his great and mighty jaw

A ſubſtance, miſcalled bone, they tore,
And faſhioned it with knife and ſaw
Into ſome dozen rods or more
        That you might ſpread.

VII.

Another monſter, who beguiled
The time by roaming India's wild
        Near Coromandel,
While gambolling upon the plain,
Deſpite, and for, his teeth was ſlain
That you for uſe, in caſe of rain,
        Might have a handle.

VIII.

Your ſilken cover, — to be brief, —
Was once a ſimple mulberry-leaf
        On mulberry-tree,
And now by proceſſes I'll not
Mention, becauſe I can't, is what
        I plainly ſee.

IX.

Many a ſhower you have braved,
And many a coat and hat you've ſaved, —
        Protecting thing!
All know there are not many ways
In which a rhymeſter ever pays

For benefits conferred, — his lays
Are ſometimes all that he can raiſe,
So reſt contented if your praiſe
I briefly ſing.

X.

I've found you through all change the ſame, —
You've ne'er deſerved that hateful name,
Fair-weather friend;
Where'er I've been, on land or ſea,
By day or night, you've ſtood by me
When ſtorms aroſe, right gallantly,
Until the end.

XI.

I prize you, though you have no beauty,
For this, that you have done your duty
As if you knew it.
Now calm and quietly you ſtand
In reach of my extended hand,
Ready, when ſuch is my command,
Again to do it.

XII.

When in a proper frame of mind
There's nought in which one cannot find
Inſtructive teaching,
That will improve him, if he'll lay it

Cloſe to his heart, and will obey it,
As much, with all reſpect I ſay it,
As pulpit preaching.

XIII.

I'll moralize, for ſoon or late,
Such is the ſtern decree of Fate,
An angel comes
With power to ſummon us away,
No choice have we to go or ſtay,
But that ſad word, Farewell, muſt ſay
To our dear homes.

XIV.

When to my life he puts the bound,
In one reſpect would I be found
Not unlike thee.
Ere yet by Death my limbs are chilled,
On this alone my hopes I build,
That when my beating heart is ſtilled
I may be thought to have fulfilled
My deſtiny.

OLD WINE IN NEW BOTTLES.

NO. I.

SAID James to John, "Pray tell me, Sir,
  Why is it that the Devil,
In ſpite of all his naughtineſs,
  Can never be uncivil?"
Then John replied, "The anſwer's plain
  To any mind that's bright,—
The *Imp o' Darkneſs* ne'er can be
  Conſidered *Imp o' Light*."

NO. II.

My Chriſtian friend, I've heard it ſaid
  The highly valued rarity,—
A perfect wife,—with Satan has
  One point of ſimilarity;
For, while in ſleep the Huſband-man
  Forgets his worldly cares,
She, to her credit be it ſaid,
  Then comes and *ſews the tears*.

NO. III.

Old Paterfamilias called to his ſide
  Little Tommy, his wonderful ſon,
And inquired, "How differs a hen with two wings
  From a hen that poſſeſſes but one?"
Then Tommy replied, for the lad in the field
  Of wit held extenſive dominion,
"The diſtinction is ſmall, for there ſeems but to be
  A ſlight difference, Sir, of *a pinion.*"

NO. IV.

Were you ever in Cork, Sir? was Foote aſked one
  day;
And the Actor replied in his humorous way,
That though in moſt cities of note he had been
Yet *of Cork* 'twas *the drawings* alone that he'd ſeen.

NO. V.

Said Johnſon, this galvanized goblet of lead
  Shall be his who can ſooneſt aſſemble
His wits, and ſay when can a candle be ſaid
  A tombſtone at all to reſemble.
Then Jackſon replied, with ſucceſsful endeavor,
  Extending his hand for the cup,
That a candle reſembles a tombſtone whenever
  'Tis for any late huſband ſet up.

NO. VI.

The Pilgrim o'er a defert wild
  Should ne'er let want confound him,
For he at any time can eat
  The *fand which is* around him.
It might feem odd that he could find
  Such palatable fare,
Did not we know the fons of *Ham*
  Were *bred* and *muftered* there.

NO. VII.

Jane fears to walk 'mid flowers in Spring,
  Though each one fragrance diftils,
Becaufe her nerves are weak, and all
  The plants are *fhooting piftils.*

NO. VIII.

a rage to the office of Counfellor B.
  Rufhed a gallant militia commander
To learn whether "Jackafs," as oft he was called,
  Was a ground for an action of flander;
The lawyer replied, "In fome cafes the term,
  If not flanderous, at leaft is pfeudonymous,
But in yours, (and for this I fhall make you no charge,)
  I confider it merely fynonymous.

NO. IX.

Blank's Poems fell on Julia's head,
Not long ſhe bore the pain ; —
The Jury found ſhe died of milk
And water on the brain.

NO. X.

I put my pen to this ſcrap of paper
To aſk if you comprehend the relation
The entry-mat bears to the outſide ſcraper ?
If you do, pleaſe reply without heſitation ;
But you don't, for your brain works exceedingly ſlow,
And you needn't ſmile in that imbecile way
When I ſay, *a ſtep farther ;* for you didn't know,
And that iſn't what you were juſt going to ſay.

NO. XI.

At church, Joe ſays, his manly heart
With true devotion ſwells ;
Diſproving that — as ſome aſſert —
He's led there by *the Belles ;*
While Jane, the happieſt of coquettes,
Whoſe eye no ſorrow dims,
Moſt piouſly employs her time
In looking for *the Hims.*

NO. XII.

When Sambo, with a bull behind,
  Of life and limb in danger,
Shuns any cloſe acquaintance with
  The rude unpleaſant ſtranger,
No doubt, like Patriots of old,
  Should fear ſtill leave him ſenſe,
He'd give, if nought for tribute, yet
  His "millions for *de fence*."

NO. XIII.

"Are there not too many *paſſages*
  In Plagiary's Play?"
"Yes, ſo many that the meaning
  Has wholly loſt its way."

NO. XIV.

The Philoſopher who ſeeks
  The fabled ſtone in vain,
Is like old Father Neptune,
  The Monarch of the Main;
For no perſon in his ſenſes
  The concluſion can reſiſt,
When I ſay, *he is a ſeeking*
  What never did exiſt.

NO. XV.

The reaſon why a bear ſhould ſeek
A dry-goods ſhop ſeems puzzling,
And ſo I'll ſtate that there he'd want
Juſt nothing elſe but *muzzling*.

NO. XVI.

Byron aſked Moore, "In Love wherein
Aught of reſemblance lies
To the potato ?" "Why ! " ſaid Moore,
"They both *ſhoot from the eyes.*"
"That anſwer's good," rejoined my Lord,
In the general laughter ſharing,
"But the likeneſs that I fancied, was,
They both *decreaſe by paring.*"

NO. XVII.

'Tis not caprice that moves the duck,
Throughout all times and ſeaſons,
To diſappear beneath the wave,
For it has *divers* reaſons ;
And its return to light and air
Caprice does not direct, —
The reaſons for this ſecond move
Are *ſundry*, I ſuſpect.

NO. XVIII.

When Johnſon for a time diſſolved
  The conjugal relation,
He told his wife he'd ſend her funds,
  Which was a conſolation ;
But ſhe at laſt was forced to ſay,
  As by the months went flitting
And nothing came, "Great kindneſs this, —
  'Tis truly *unremitting*."

NO. XIX.

Luck varies with the men who hunt
  For gold, as I'll explain :
Some find the ore *in creaſes*,
  While others ſeek *in vein*.

NO. XX.

Knoweſt thou, whene'er the joyleſs mind
  Seems moſt diſtraught with grief,
Where ſympathy the heart can find,
  And genuine relief ?
If not, then Reader, learn from me,
  Howe'er the caſes vary,
You'll find *Relief* and *Sympathy*
  In every Dictionary.

NO. XXI.

Once, at a feaſt, when jokes flew 'round
  Much thicker than the flies,
The hoſt had doubts if he ſhould carve
  The mutton *ſaddlewiſe*,
And therefore turned to Theodore Hook,
  The celebrated Wit,
Who anſwered, "*Bridlewiſe*, for in
  My mouth will be a *bit*."

NO. XXII.

Forth from the Opera I ſaw a wag,
  Well known to Fame in all his glory come,
And as he ſtepped upon the icy flag
  He fell with force enough to ſtrike him dumb,
And rolling over, landed in the gutter;
  I ſprang to ſave,—but only caught his hat,—
And as he roſe I thought I heard him mutter,
  "One muſt *C ſharp* if he would not *B flat*."

NO. XXIII.

QUESTION.

Fair Joan of Arc, they ſay, was not
  Sword, lance or pike afraid of;
Can any perſon tell me what
  So brave a girl was made of?

ANSWER.

The Heroine, whoſe triumphant blade
  Made Bedford's ſoldiers dance,
If Hiſtory tells the truth, was Maid
  Of Orleans, in France.

SONNETS.

Like an indulgent mother, Nature ſtill
Awaits her prodigal's return ; — nor blame
Nor ſcorn has ſhe, but ever ſmiles the ſame
And yields her bounties to each one who will ;
Her generous arms ſhe opes to him who worn
With toil and ſorrow, hopeleſs and forlorn,
Jaded and fainting with the unceaſing ſtrife
And battle with the world, would ſeek for reſt, —
Enfolds him like an infant to her breaſt
And reads him leſſons of a purer life.
Here, with this ſtreamlet rippling at my feet,
Far from the roar and turmoil of the town,
I feel the rapture of her preſence ſweet,
Nor would reſign it for an Emperor's crown.

As ſome poor captive, priſoned and enchained,
Who long in vain has ſtruggled to be free,
Will learn to deem his lot by Heaven ordained
And yield to what he thought a ſtern decree,
So I, rebellious once, now can but bleſs
The fate that makes me ſo entirely thine,
To love and ſerve thee is my happineſs ; —
Who would be free where bondage is divine !
In joy and grief, in pleaſure and in pain,
Neareſt and deareſt to thy heart I've ſtood ;
'Tis mockery to say, "Be free once more,"
My arm is powerleſs to ope the door
Would lead me forth ; — ſo long I've worn thy chain
I could not break it, Deareſt, if I would.

WITHOUT, the tempeſt rages, and the winds
Howl like unearthly ſpirits through the ſtreet,
My caſements ſhake in concert with the blinds,
And all the panes are cruſted o'er with ſleet;
But here within is comfort and repoſe,
The cheerful logs are blazing on my hearth, —
Of favorite books in rows ſucceeding rows,
That ſtand at my command, there is no dearth;
Theſe are the valued friends with whom I live, —
Friends who aſſume no privilege to ſay
Unwelcome truths, or mark my faults, or give
Unaſked advice, — right pleaſant friends are they.
With them, — this pipe, — that flaſk of Rheniſ
wine, —
Though tempeſts rage, — beatitude is mine.

I PINE and languiſh with deſire to know
Something of this unquiet heart of mine,
The myſtery of its life, and where ſhall flow
In future time this eſſence ſo divine,—
Soul, Spirit, Mind, Intelligence, or Love,
Or whatſoe'er,—that raiſes me above
The brutes that wholly die; and whence aroſe
The ſpark that lighted in my heart this fire.
As Life is haſtening on, more fiercely glows
Within me this unſatisfied deſire
Heaven's book of knowledge in my hands to graſp
And all the bonds of Ignorance unclaſp;
But I muſt wait God's time,—then each ſhall know
Whence his life came and whither it ſhall go.

In genial ſunſhine and in ſtormy weather
O'er pleaſant ſlopes and through ſome rugged ways,
E'en from the earlieſt of our boyhood's days,
We two have walked Life's varied path together,
And ſhall we now, in ſpite of what hath been
Through all theſe years, ignore the well-knit band
Of fellowſhip? Aloof ſhall we two ſtand
While wider grows the gulf that yawns between,
Until its hollow jaws ſhall ope ſo wide
That all endeavor will be vain to croſs, —
While we regret, too late, each other's loſs, —
And all for cheriſhing a fooliſh pride?
No. Not if one atoning word of mine
Sent from my heart hath power to meet with thine.

As ſome light bark upon a ſummer ſea
Holding its homeward courſe, with hope elate
And joy triumphant, ſpeeding gallantly,
Unconſcious of its ſad impending fate,
Is ſuddenly by Jove's dread lightning riven,
Then, wrecked and ſhattered, by the tempeſt driven;
So my confiding heart, that day by day
Seemed haſtening to the haven of its reſt
Where Care and Sorrow ne'er ſhould find their way,
But Love and Happineſs would build their neſt,
Was ſtricken by a fatal blow, and hurled
Again upon a cold and heartleſs world;
Hope, as ſhe fled me, whiſpered all was loſt,
And now my heart is wrecked and tempeſt-toſt.

THERE is an Art no penalties engird,
Of power tranſcendent, — ever in our reach, —
And our own hearts its daily need can teach ;
No laws reſtrict its uſe, — to all 'tis free
As Heaven's great gift of air ; the vulgar herd
Have equal rights with Kings ; and yet 'tis ſtrange,
Knowing its limitleſs extent of range,
So few employ its magic miniſtry.
Its ſway o'er young and old no voice can ſpeak, —
It hath a charm to change the wayward mood
Of friends and lovers, — to ſuſtain the weak, —
To tame the brutal, — to reſtrain the rude, —
To win the wandering, and to ſoothe diſtress.
'Tis Love's own graceful Art of Gentleneſs.

THE knell is tolled of all my joyous dreams
Of tranquil happineſs, my Love, with thee.
And all the Future, once ſo brilliant, teems
With nought but lonelineſs and miſery;
For Hope lies buried, — funeral tapers burn
Where Hymen's torch ſhould throw its gladdening
beams.
Dark ſhadows greet me whereſoe'er I turn,
And ſeem to mock me with a fiendiſh glee, —
No reſignation can my ſpirit learn, —
No conſolation can Time bring to me; —
A barren ſpot whereon no ſunſhine gleams, —
A wreck abandoned on a ſtormy ſea, —
A withered garland on ſepulchral urn, —
Are what my heart is like, apart from thee.

ADVICE is wafted both by Sage and Preacher
Becaufe Experience ever keeps the fchool
Wherein all learn, — the wife man and the fool;
Whate'er men fay, fhe is the only teacher,
Her tafks are hard, — her leffons, flowly learned,
Are ne'er forgotten; deeply are they burned
Into the very foul. Ah, yes! and when
In later years our felf-conceit departs,
And, if at all, true wifdom comes to men,
A confcioufnefs of folly fills our hearts;
The mifts that fhroud our vifion break away
And then to our regret we clearly fee
What vain illufions lured our fteps aftray; —
How falfe the Gods to which we bent the knee.

Is there no balm in Gilead for the mood
Wherein I ſit in miſery, and feel
Anew the agony Time will not heal?
In hopeleſſneſs, deſpair, and grief I brood,
My heart conſuming in this ſolitude,
Groping in darkneſs, — ſeeking but in vain
For comfort to this mourning ſoul of mine;
Hath Friendſhip's gentle craft no anodyne
To ſoothe the trouble of an o'erwrought brain?
Alas! No miniſtry of human art, —
Whate'er its miſſion in this world of pain, —
Can cure the deſolation of the heart;
But Faith, that bids us never to deſpond,
Can rend the gloom and ſhow the Heaven beyond.

In this delicious ſilence ſo profound
Of Night's moſt halcyon hour, as I lie
Stretched on the turf beneath a gorgeous ſky
While all the world is huſhed, am I not crowned
With Heaven's divineſt gift, — a joyous heart?
All paſſions ceaſe, — no evil thought can mar
The glory ſhed on me by moon and ſtar, —
The world's vexations one by one depart,
The wounds of daily ſuffering are healed, —
Long-cheriſhed hatreds, and all ſenſe of wrong
Held in my inmoſt ſoul I freely yield; —
For perfect Love, e'en ſuch as Poet's ſong
Hath never told, ſo fills this heart of mine,
I know the Preſence near me is Divine.

BEFORE my voice is ſilent with the dead,
Would I might breathe one grand and noble lay
That, — ſung beſide the dying ſufferer's bed, —
Would ſoothe the fainting ſoul and aching head, —
Teach my ſad brethren on their onward way
To ſtruggle manfully from day to day, —
Inſpire a firmer truſtfulneſs, — relieve
The bitter agony of thoſe who grieve, —
Rouſe the deſpairing, — and make cold hearts beat
With a ſublime emotion. I would give
All of this life in human hearts to live.
Grant me to ſing that ſong divinely ſweet,
Then 'neath the daiſies joyfully I'll lie
For I ſhall know I cannot wholly die.

L'ENVOI.

TO THE READER.

My wiſh is granted, if the paſſing hour
That thou haſt given to theſe, — my ſmiles and
tears, —
Should have by happy chance the magic power
As friends to leave us for the coming years ;
It may be ſo, if aught from heart of mine
Hath touched a chord that vibrated in thine.

www.ingramcontent.com/pod-product-compliance
Lightning Source LLC
LaVergne TN
LVHW021409110826
845150LV00007B/1847

* 9 7 8 1 4 2 5 5 1 1 4 1 8 *